Sex
&
SANDWICHES

by
Tracey L. DeBrew

Kathy:
It's okay to 'eat' in
the bedroom! ☺

Tracey DeBrew

herwritehand publishing, Inc
Washington, DC

Paperback First Edition 2011

Library of Congress Cataloging Number
available upon request

ISBN-13: (Pbk)
978-0-9832492-0-7

to Mom & Dad-

thanks for encouraging me to write at all times

"Love is the answer, but while you're waiting for the answer, sex raises some pretty good questions." – Woody Allen

CHAPTER 1

He giggled boyishly and then pressed his lips firmly against my opened mouth to keep me quiet until he was done. I could feel my back slide up and down against the bathroom mirror while I was perched on the counter with Ian's arms wrapped firmly around me. The oncoming explosion that was about to erupt between my thighs was briefly diverted as I thought to myself, *I'm going to be late again.*

If only I hadn't let Ian throw my leg over his shoulder while I was trying to brush my teeth this morning, I wouldn't be in this mess in the first place. All I could think about was the look that everyone would have on their faces when I walked into that conference room — fifteen, maybe twenty minutes late. I can just read the glances. I will be labeled a sex-craved failure — the single woman who couldn't keep her act up long enough to get the job done. It was disheartening to know that the whole world looked at me through a magnifying glass. Well, maybe not the whole world, just the executives in my office. All of them are nothing more than a bunch of money-hungry piranhas.

My boyfriend Ian is a nymphomaniac. He just can't get enough of me. Truth be told, I can't get enough of him either, so I suppose that makes me a nympho too? He is the type of guy who does everything I like sexually. That is a rare quality among men and I'm fortunate to have found him. He is a true gem amongst the piles of shattered rubble that I used to encounter daily. I would often find myself smiling during the day as I reminisced about the gentle way he touched me; so erotically on the curve of my hips, or the hungry look he would give me just before pleasing me.

I'm late and I have no time to ponder over our random sexual escapades.

My shoe flopped haphazardly against my heel as my laptop bag rhythmically slapped my side while I hobbled down the brick-laden sidewalk. My shoe, which begged to be kicked for a field goal, forced me to stop and fix it before taking another step. Some strange man walking toward me took the liberty of stealing a glance at my legs as I fastened the ankle strap in place. When I looked up at him, he brandished an awkward smile to which I rolled my eyes up toward the tall buildings that seemed to stretch toward the sun as they asked to be kissed. Just after I showed that act of disgust, my designer sheer stockings began to run right down the front of my thigh. The run raced toward my knee before I stood up straight in a poor attempt to cease its sprint. *Great*, I thought. *Ten dollar hose that run just like the three dollar ones.*

When I got to 1121 Eye Street, I pushed my way through the revolving door to gain entry. I unlocked my office and threw my items across the desk, some of which hit the floor before I could turn and head out toward the conference room. I managed to steal a few deep breaths to calm my rapidly beating heart before I turned the knob on the door. Why today? The Chairman was here to listen to this proposal.

Just before I walked in, a co-worker tapped me on the shoulder a second before I dropped them with disappointment.

"The meeting has been rescheduled for Monday."

*   *   *   *

When I got home from a long, uneventful day of work, I was surprised to see that Ian already made dinner for us. He was so sweet to me. As far as looks go, his face looked alright, but his body was a work of art. His butt was so firm that if he sat down on the sidewalk, it would be imprinted in the concrete.

After we stuffed our faces on his immaculately prepared dinner, he sat on the couch and I lay perpendicular to him, settling my buttocks in the trench of his lap.

"Ah, baby," I said with a satisfied sigh and a light pat of my stomach, "that was great."

He began massaging my legs and thighs and I knew what that meant. It meant after his food was partially digested, he wanted to fool around in the bedroom. Or maybe some other corner of the house. He was always full of surprises and had the stamina of ten men.

"I'm glad you liked it."

"Where did you learn how to cook like that?" I asked him as I stroked his bicep.

"Just something I knew I had to do. Gotta eat, may as well eat good, right?" He proved his point as his hands moved further up my thigh.

"Do you ever get enough?"

"Josephine, my darling, never!" He placed his hand behind my head and planted a wet kiss on my mouth. My back arched to allow the shivers that started from the nape of my neck to trickle down to my lower spine.

His kisses covered my mouth, ears and neck. He reached his hand down my shirt and began softly kneading my breast. I caressed the back of his head as it nuzzled my chest. I wanted to relax for the evening, but Ian had a way of jumpstarting all of my hot buttons. His foreplay was hypnotic. I felt like he was a puppeteer, and my heart, mind and body dangled by a string.

Right there on the couch, I straddled him and feasted upon his butterscotch-colored skin. He lifted his arms prompting me to lift his shirt that revealed a stomach so chiseled it could grate cheddar. His shoulders were stirrups that I delicately would be resting the backs of my ankles against once he tore me out of my clothes. Still straddling him, he lifted me and we headed to the rear of the house in the direction of the deck. It was dark with the exception of the moonlight that bounced against the sliding glass door.

We stepped outside and my feet refused to be placed solidly on the wooden planks due to the chill. He gently pressed my back against the cool aluminum siding causing my nipples to perk. He feasted upon those as I looked out hazily into the wooded area that the deck faced.

My stomach rumbled and it felt like it was trying to digest a tennis ball that was gradually expanding. My stuffed stomach swelled and my libido instantly deflated. I tried to push him away by his shoulders. I was unable to speak as I began to break out in a sweat. My eyes rolled around lazily in my head as I slammed it gently against the side of the house. I looked up at the stars that seemed to be engulfed in a dance against the dark curtain of the night sky.

Unable to ignore the onslaught of illness any longer, I pushed Ian away and dashed toward the bathroom, almost losing my balance along the way. I squatted down on the floor, lifted the lid to the porcelain receptacle and began to heave, what felt like my innards, out.

"Oh, God," I managed between breaths.

Ian stumbled inside the bathroom bare-chested as he looked down at me. He rubbed his stomach, I guess to calm it from hearing ounces of fluid being dispelled from someone else's body. He leaned his head against the doorframe for a second and then knelt beside me.

"Get outta here," I softly demanded.

"Was it the food?"

"Get out. This is gross," I pleaded. "I'll be out in a second."

Respecting what felt like my final wishes, he slowly crept out and stretched out on the couch. I heard the television come to life along with the newscaster's corny segue jokes in between toilet flushes.

When I was done, I lifted myself up, went to the sink, splashed water on my face and swished some around in my mouth, along with some mouthwash. I patted my face dry with a towel, brushed my hair back with my hands and started into the living room. He looked up at me and made space for me on the couch. I curled up to him like a little child.

"*That* made me lose my hard on," he said plainly.

"I'm sorry."

"Did you eat something from earlier that didn't agree with you?" he asked as he caressed my arm that rested across his stomach.

"No, Ian."

"Well, what's wrong, baby?"
"I'm late."
"Late for what?"
"No, baby. I'm *late*."

CHAPTER 2

I met up with Hailey at the gym. I basically just sat back and observed her rigorous regimen of cardio exercises and weightlifting. I wasn't about to strain anything just yet because I was unsure of my condition. When I explained to her what happened last night with Ian and me, and the possibility of me being pregnant, she almost dropped an eight-pound dumbbell on my foot.

"What?" she blurted.

"Keep your voice down," I said as I carefully climbed onto one of the stationary bikes. I figured a slow pedal wouldn't hurt me.

"I remember one time when I thought I was pregnant and I told Steve. He damn near broke up with me. The bastard."

"Not Steve?"

"Yes . . . Steve. I couldn't believe it." Hailey was obviously still salty about the episode because she threw the dumbbell to the floor and murmured a few expletives.

Hailey took a huge swig of water from her economy-sized jug. She had a slim frame and worked out regularly. Most of the women in the gym rolled their eyes at her whenever she worked out, but she didn't care. She would just handle her business and then leave. I could understand why after all this time Hailey was still upset with Steve not being happy about her possible pregnancy. Hailey and Steve have been dating longer than Adam and Eve. I don't know if she became content and decided to hold out for a wedding ring, or if Steve was waiting for someone better — someone better that Steve would never find. Hailey had a great job, a great personality, she was educated, looked awesome and, most importantly, she tolerated all of Steve's flaws when most other women would've dropped him in two heartbeats. Who else would put up with his mess?

Steve isn't an incredibly bad guy, he's just slow as hell and I can't quite understand why he isn't racing down the aisle to keep Hailey. Perhaps he was waiting for her to turn into some sort of superhero or something. On the other hand, Hailey didn't nag him about popping the question, which may be one of the reasons why Steve hadn't proposed yet. Hailey was quick to silence me along with her other friends when the subject of marriage came up. Her reply would always be, "I'm not thinking about that right now." You know, maybe she wasn't concerned about cultivating a future with Steve, but I couldn't help but wonder if underneath it all there was a problem with their relationship. So being the nosey friend that I am, every few months I would go against her wishes and bring it up — coincidentally, this month just so happens to be the month to inquire about the seriousness of their tenure together. Therefore, I decided to ask just to fulfill my quota.

"Hey? You and Steve go ring shopping yet?"

"What are you talking about, girl? Steve and I are kicking it."

"No offense, but you guys been *kicking it* since the Israelites crossed the Red Sea. What's up with that?"

Hailey let out an audible sigh as she prepared to stretch before finalizing her workout. "You really want to know why I'm not pressing marriage with him? Is that it?"

"Well . . . yeah," I confessed.

"You sure?"

"Positive," I confirmed.

"Girl, it's because I'm seeing someone else," she said coolly, as if I should've known that was the reason all along.

"What?!" I boomed.

"Now that's between you and me, ya' hear?"

I nodded like a five-year old being told that being a tattletale was a very bad thing.

"So hold up," I said with a raised palm, "who's this other guy?"

Hailey continued stretching as she took a while to answer; so long that I thought she didn't hear my question. When I was about to repeat it, she let out a huge sigh and walked toward one side of the bike next to me and looked me square in the eye.

"You already know too much. The less info you have, the better. Steve can take his time. While he's waiting, I'm getting laid like a Persian carpet."

*   *   *   *

Bryan Bryant was one of the hottest columnists at the Washington Post newspaper. He had written two books, so quite naturally he thought his "you know what" didn't stink. Bryan was a clean-cut guy, who sort of fell in the middle as far as looks. From a distance he could get a few stares, up close he looked nice, but after one studied his face, he just looked alright.

To put it bluntly, Bryan Bryant used to be a "nobody" at *The Post*, but now that he was finally being noticed, his career was zooming toward the stratosphere. He even had a bullshit cameo on some unpopular show on UPN.

One of my friends, Camilla, met him and was able to penetrate his "I'm a star" bubble that surrounded him. Since then, she has not been able to shut up about him and she was positive that this man was definitely Mr. Right. I wasn't sure what exactly she noticed about him first — the right pocket or his left one.

Camilla was a sweet girl, but she was a groupie through and through. She often made her way to all of the Wizards and Redskins after parties and always booked a year ahead for any star-studded awards show just to see which single celebrity she could meet. I wasn't mad at her because girlfriend was definitely on a mission to settle down with some rich guy before she turned 30.

One evening Camilla thought it would be a phenomenal idea if Ian and I met her and Bryan for dinner. Ian immediately declined.

"Hell naw! I ain't meeting his snobby ass nowhere," Ian said before propping his feet up on the coffee table.

However, being the nosey person that I am, I wanted to see how Bryan and Camilla interacted. If he was really the jerk that his peers claimed him to be, and if my instincts told me whether or not their relationship was going anywhere.

Although I could only speculate, I suspected that Bryan probably had many women at his beck and call every day of the week.

The three of us had dinner at this snazzy spot on The Hill — the hip nickname for Capitol Hill.

"So Camilla tells me you're in advertising," Bryan said. He perched his jaw against his Adam's apple while he spoke. His Shakespearean-like voice lowered a few octaves and he looked over his glasses when he addressed me. I despised his actions right from the start. He seemed like some stuffed shirt from Harvard, when his used-to-be broke ass went to community college.

I decided to play along more so to mock him than anything else. Right then I made up my mind to be completely fake at first, and then progressively get real with him instead of just being fake all night. It would be less boring for me, that was for sure, but highly embarrassing for Camilla. I'm sure with time she would get over it.

"Yes, and it's too bad you've already promoted both of your books! If you write a third, give us a jingle!" I said before I mustered up a stifled giggle and sipped my white wine.

Camilla was instantly annoyed with me because she sensed I may have been trying to sabotage the evening with my phoniness. She shot a damning look at me without Bryan seeing, to which I returned a wink and a smirk to upset her even more. In response to our non-verbal exchange, she sharply snapped her linen napkin in the air and spread it out over her lap. It took every ounce of restraint that I could congregate just so I would not be inclined to laugh at them both.

"That I am. I am working on a third one," he admitted.

I wanted to turn the attention off of me for the rest of the night. This gathering was not supposed to be about me and my job, but about Bryan's job, his future and how Camilla would fit in to it.

"So how long have you and Camilla been dating?" I asked him.

Bryan looked at Camilla seriously and narrowed his eyes as he tried to remember. This was not a good sign. Camilla wore a stupid grin on her face to show him that she would be patient as he answered my question. However, I knew what that grin meant. It meant, *You've been sleeping with me, but don't know how long you've been doing it?* Once again, I had to suppress the urge to burst into laughter.

"Not that I need an exact date, just a round about," I tried to help ease the pressure I put on Bryan.

"What? About a month or so?" he quietly asked.

"No," Camilla told him sternly. "Four."

"Wow, so it's at that 'this is getting serious' mark, huh?" I held up air quotes to emphasize the getting serious part. I was intently prying into their personal business, but, hell, we needed to know these things. Truth be told, I was just getting started with my interrogation.

Simultaneously they both answered. Except Camilla said, "Yes," and Bryan said "No." Strike two. I was on a roll. Camilla fired a condemning look at Bryan, who blatantly ignored it. By now Camilla had enough of my shenanigans and abruptly tossed her napkin onto the table. She then boldly announced that she needed to go to the little girls' room.

"Josephine, come with?" she asked politely, which was not like her *at all*.

Camilla was putting on an act for Bryan just as much as he was putting on one for me. It was no wonder those two lasted for four months because they both were putting up a front.

"No, you go on ahead," I shooed her with my hand. "I can stay and get better acquainted with Mr. Bryant."

Camilla stood by the table and refused to leave until I joined her. When I didn't get the hint, she made up some excuse.

"This thing has been scratching my back," she said as she awkwardly contorted her arm around her back to show that she could not reach the area that nagged her. From her demonstration, clearly she required assistance.

"Excuse me, Bryan," I said and popped up from the table.

"Certainly," he added for good measure.

When we entered the restroom, I tried to figure out what stitch of fabric, tag, or whatever was nagging her by placing my hand on the area. She spun around wildly and faced me. The air from her pirouette grazed my face.

"Can you believe him? And just what the hell are you doing?" she fired at me.

"What? What are you talking about?"

"Don't grill him," she pleaded.

"Girl, come on," I coaxed. "I'm doing you a huge favor. I'm asking all of the questions you can't. That's the whole point of having me here. Since he *is* answering them, you can't tell me you aren't the least bit surprised by his answers."

"Stop it! Bryan Bryant is about to blow up even more and I want to be the woman on his arm when he does!"

"Okay, Camilla. You are scaring me."

"Josephine, this guy is awesome. . ."

I furrowed my brows and was about to shake my head before she tacked on an addendum to her comment.

". . . on paper. He's awesome on paper. I mean, he may not be the most handsome guy in the world, but right now he's got it going on. He's perfect for me right now."

"Right now?" For a moment I thought she was completely free of all her senses. "What are you saying? Are you listening to yourself? Do you know what you sound like?"

She shook her head totally clueless.

"You know what? You sound like a gold digger," I flat out told her.

Camilla shrugged a shoulder and looked over at her image in the mirror.

"Camilla, let me tell you, this dude came up from nothing. Now, I'm happy for his success, but I get the feeling he doesn't know how to handle it. Just watch yourself. You may think you are playing him, but don't end up being the one who's getting played." I placed a comforting hand on her shoulder. "Now, let me go back out there and finish acting phony. After the main course, I will unleash the ghetto, hard knock side!" I laughed, did a jiggle and headed out of the restroom. I could hear Camilla sniggling behind me.

When Camilla and I returned to the table, our entrées had arrived. They were tiny portions placed strategically in the middle of the plate, with different colored sauces splattered neatly over the white porcelain. A huge sprig of rosemary was shoved into whatever I ordered. I thought I ordered grilled salmon, but it looked like a slice of Jimmy Dean sausage. It was obvious that I would be ordering something from the dollar menu at some burger joint on the way home. What a jip. Fifty-five dollars for three, maybe four bites of food? For that amount of money, this better be one hell of a tasty sausage-looking piece of fish. I can't believe I skipped lunch for this.

My disgust regarding the serving portion spilled over onto Bryan. Someone needed to feel my rage and since I didn't know him that well, he would be the unsuspecting victim.

"So Bryan, do you plan on getting married soon or are you more of a free spirit?"

Camilla's shoe grazed mine. She tried to kick me a second time, but I slid my leg out of the way so instead she ended up kicking the table very hard.

"Ow! Excuse me," was all she could say. I laughed on the inside and made a personal note to laugh out loud about it once I got into my car to head home. Instead of having a giggling frenzy right then and there, I ignored her and waited for Bryan's response.

"Maybe a little of both," he responded coolly. "I don't plan on getting married soon, but someday."

"Camilla is a very nice catch," I added.

Instead of her trying to kick me this time, she shoved my arm and giggled with embarrassment. Bryan kept slicing his entrée that looked a bit like a miniature chicken plank from Long John Silver's. After he popped the bite of food into his mouth, he began looking at the other patrons in the restaurant, obviously bored with our company.

Camilla giggled even louder this time before she offered something in response to my comment.

"Josephine, please. You're putting Bryan on the spot."

"No, she's not," he said.

Well, and on that note, that was strike three. Bryan clearly was not interested in a future with Camilla. He neglected to respond to my observation regarding her. Either he didn't hear what I said or he flat out ignored the comment. The restaurant was in no way noisy and I was not soft-spoken, so my guess was the latter. If he was in any way interested in Camilla, he had a weird way of showing it. Then again, for him four months may have been too early to tell.

Poor Camilla. I guess it is back to the after parties.

CHAPTER 3

For the past few weeks I barely saw my other girlfriend, Tamar. She told me that she was working hard on getting her well-deserved promotion at work. Hopefully all of those long hours, company outings and schmoozing will pay off for her. She and I were a lot alike with one exception, well, one big exception — she loved having sex with men she barely knew. She explained that it was much less committal accompanied with little to no drama. She tried the long-term relationship thing before, but despite her efforts to make it successful, she was astonished to discover that the relationship she labored over just ended up being unhealthy and unstable. In fact, that one relationship caused her so much turmoil that she never wanted to talk about it. As a result, she turned off her emotions when it came to dealing with men. According to her, she could have her sexual way with them and vice versa, kick them out, or if she was at their place, leave without feeling any attachments. "It's the only way to fly," she would say.

Finally the day came at her job where her boss would announce the newest partner to the law firm. Her boss entered. He was a man in his mid-forties who had begun to develop what would most likely become the worst comb-over in balding history. Almost everyday, despite the professional dress code, he wore those three-button, cotton pullovers that were usually stained with coffee. The green, gaping-mouthed alligator patch on the left breast of his shirt was just centimeters from getting his thirst quenched. His outdated boat shoes had ripped leather laces and the brownish color was faded and deteriorated.

"Well," he began as he slapped a file down on his desk. The small gust of air slightly lifted Tamar's swept bang. She nervously rubbed the arms of the wooden chair as she glanced at his photos of *Biggest Fish Caught* contests, his bedraggled wife and two God-forsaken bratty kids that came and took the office by storm. Tamar still couldn't find her treasured *Looney Tunes* figurine collection. Those little thieves!

"I've thought a lot about this, Tamar."

"Not too hard, I hope," she chuckled because she did not like his apologetic tone. All he had to do was tell her she had made partner of the firm.

"We've decided to hold off on announcing partner and hired someone from outside the organization."

Tamar's jaw landed in her lap.

"He's very qualified and I know that you will enjoy working with him," the boss smiled rottenly.

"Hold it. *I'm* very qualified," Tamar emphasized her statement by pointing to herself.

The wooden chair skidded across the carpet as Tamar pushed it back and prepared to stand. She placed her hand on her hip and pointed her finger at him to indicate that the cursing was about to commence. Just as she was about to unleash every degrading expletive known to man before quitting her job, her boss' office door opened.

"Ah! Here he is now. Donovan Jacobs, meet Tamar Woodruff. You two will be working very closely together."

Tamar spun around quickly, her mouth pouted and eyes narrowed in preparation to shoot a thousand or so daggers. Donovan stood about six feet two inches, with a flawless complexion and broad shoulders. His smile showed off his straight, white teeth and a single deep dimple. His long lashes preceded his big, brown eyes. Donovan extended his masculine hand for Tamar to shake, while he slyly looked her up and down.

Tamar stared at the inviting hand, looked back at her boss who was grinning stupidly, and then looked back to Donovan. Instinctively she scoffed, threw a single hand up in surrender, brushed past Donovan and left the office.

Tamar stomped down the hallway and jabbed the down arrow for the elevator to deliver her to the foyer so she could remove herself from that building. She had no idea where she was going and she didn't take the time to grab her purse from her cube. She just wanted out and had no intentions of coming back until she felt calm enough. On the busy street below she intended to scream in frustration as loud as her lungs would allow. There was no way that she was going to take more orders from someone else for another two years without recompense.

After everything I've done for this place! Tamar thought to herself. She stabbed the down arrow again because the elevator was taking entirely too long in her estimation. She paced in front of the hesitant elevator with her arms folded tightly across her body. Agitated, she huffed loudly and slammed her back against the wall just opposite the elevator doors.

"Hurry up," she mumbled with frustration. With that order, the bell chimed and the elevator opened.

"Tamar?" she heard a voice say before she stepped onto the elevator. She was not about to entertain anyone at the moment, she just wanted a few moments of freedom. The doors were about to close, but a familiar hand caught it before they snapped shut to make their descent. Donovan stepped inside and plastered the same backstabbing smile he mustered in the boss' office just moments ago.

As the doors were closing, Tamar leaned to one side, crossed her arms and dared him to make her an ally. They were all alone and could talk freely.

"I know this is probably devastating for you, Tamar, but I think together our ideas and hard work will bring a new energy to the office. I'll do what I can to get you that partnership that you deserve, but I'm going to need some help."

"Help?"

"Yes."

A chime sounded to signal that the elevator reached the lobby. Tamar stepped out and turned to face him with a slight smirk formed upon her lips.

"If you need help, dial 911."

With that tidbit of advice, Tamar watched as the concern that Donovan displayed on the elevator ride down became drained from his entire being. After she saw the hurt in his eyes, the doors closed.

CHAPTER 4

Ian drove me to the doctor so we could officially find out if I was pregnant or not. I haven't been having an appetite and wasn't able to keep what little food I ate in my stomach. Although my "monthly bill" finally showed up, a few of my friends said to still get the test taken.

At times, Ian seemed happy about the fact that I may be pregnant, and at other times it was hard to read what he was thinking. For instance, most mornings he normally gives me oral pleasure. Today, instead, he turned his back to me, gave a huge sigh and drifted back off to sleep for a few more minutes. When I jostled him in bed, with my deliberate stirring as I pretended to get comfortable, he sucked his teeth and popped up to go to the bathroom. He stayed in there for about twenty minutes. When the door opened, he grabbed a towel from the linen closet and started his shower. Talk about me being disappointed.

No licky licky, I thought to myself.

We made our way to the doctor's office and said no more than about ten words to each other for the entire trip. I'm positively sure that if he was unhappy about this pregnancy it was because he was more concerned with how our sex life would be, or even if there would be one, if I were pregnant. We've talked about getting married and having kids, so I know he would be happy to have a son. However, I'm almost certain that the nine-month wait would damn near kill him sexually.

"Okay, we ran all of the necessary tests," the doctor told us as he flopped down in his high-back leather chair.

Ian reached over and squeezed my hand gently as we both looked eagerly at the doctor for what the results would be. Whenever I sat and would get nervous, I would cross my legs and wiggle my foot about as fast as a hummingbird's wings fluttered. Just then, unbeknownst to me, my foot started wiggling. Ian released his hand from mine and laid it across my knee to get me to relax and cease all of that foot wiggling.

"Are we going to be parents?" Ian asked the doctor.

"I'm sorry. No," the doctor pressed his lips together to show his compassion. "The test came back negative. I believe your vomiting spell may have occurred from a virus. I've written a prescription that should help work it out of your system. Give it about three days, but keep taking the medicine until you've finished the bottle. I'm sorry."

I looked down at my lap and then at Ian's hand that caressed mine gently.

"Thank you, doctor," Ian said as I tried to smile. As we both stood, Ian took my hand and led me back toward the waiting room.

Ian and I did not exchange words as we waited for my prescription to be filled. For a second there, I thought I was actually going to be a mother. I didn't know how to take Ian's silence — as relief or disappointment. I know he cared for me deeply, but we never really had "the talk." We mentioned marriage and how our kids would be in a few casual conversations, but we never really sat down to map out everything pertaining to our future. Honestly, taking our relationship to the next level wasn't something that I had given *that* much thought. Don't get me wrong, I wanted to be with Ian and there was no question from me about us being together. I suppose I just assumed we would be.

When we loaded ourselves into the car, I just stared blankly out of the window. I didn't know what to say to Ian. I was unsure how I felt about it myself. The news from the doctor was still sinking in, so to speak. Today our time spent in the car was different. Normally, we would've listened to some music that would be turned up so loudly it could shatter all of the windows. Today, we drove in a deafening silence.

When we were almost to his house he cleared his throat, disturbing the stillness in the car. Afterward, he spoke up.

"Josephine?" he said coolly.

"Yes?"

"You... really wanted to have *my* child?" he placed his warm hand over my knee.

"Why do you ask like it's hard to believe?" I looked at him for the first time during the drive home.

"It kinda is. I mean, I guess I didn't really know how you felt about me."

"What? You can't be serious."

"I mean, I know you care about me, but enough to want to have my child? No, I didn't know that. That means a lot to me, baby."

I couldn't think of anything to say at that point, so I patted his hand, gave him a smile and looked back out of the window. He gave a heavy sigh and nervously cleared his throat again before he spoke.

"So, uh, how soon do you take the medicine?"

"Oh, I hadn't even thought about it. I guess I should take it this evening with dinner."

"Okay, then I guess I'll cook your favorite."

I smiled and looked at him again. "My favorite? That's not something that you make all the time."

"I know, but you deserve it. I'll drop you off at the house and pick up the stuff from the grocery store."

"You are so sweet to me, Ian." I leaned over and kissed his cheek.

"Well, you're my woman, aren't you?"

Like the special meal he would be preparing this evening, his comment was not something he said very often. In fact, he *never* mentioned it. It was just this unwritten rule we had, I guess. We always gave each other space, but enjoyed each other's company as well. Maybe Ian *was* a bit disappointed with the fact of not becoming a father just yet.

I propped my feet up on the couch and watched the evening news, while Ian fixed my favorite meal. It didn't take him long to prepare. When I got bored with the city's mayhem and crimes being reported on the news, I repositioned myself on the couch and tried to read a few magazine articles. My eyes passed over the words and I really hadn't comprehended what I was reading. I could hear Ian retrieving some clean dishes from the dishwasher and placing the food on them. He placed the prepared plates on a serving tray and carted them out to me.

"Here you go," he said as he handed me the plate. "Your favorite."

"Thanks, Ian! This means so much!" I took the plate with a huge grin plastered on my face and was ready to dig in.

"*Sloppy Joes a la Ian,*" he announced.

I took a huge bite out of the sandwich as most of the filling spilled out of the bun. Ian made so many exotic meals, most of which I had never had while growing up, that it seemed that the simplest, messiest meals were also usually the most filling. In fact, Ian didn't just brown the ground beef and pour a can of sauce over it, his Sloppy Joes were definitely gourmet. I guess he just couldn't help himself when it came to cooking everything at its best.

As I took a few more bites, I glanced over at Ian's plate. It was clean! He was wiping his mouth with a napkin and guzzling down his ginger ale. I think that man finished his sandwich in four bites. While I was still working on mine, he wanted to talk about what happened this afternoon.

"Josephine, did you just want a baby, or *my* baby?"

Not believing what I was still hearing, I covered my Sloppy Joe filled mouth with a napkin when I answered him. "Why are you asking me that?"

"Well, it's just something I need to know. You never really answered that in the car earlier."

"I care about you very much. You are a sweet guy . . ."

"But?"

After I wiped my mouth with the napkin, I scoffed at his negativity and then threw it at him.

"There *are* no buts. You are one of the nicest, kindest, most sex-crazed men I've ever met. I would've been very happy if I was carrying your child."

"Really? I mean, you could have any guy and I know I'm not the finest brother in the world . . ."

"To me, you are."

I set the plate down on the coffee table and placed my hand on his cheek. He looked down in his lap before he placed his hand over mine and kissed the inside of it. He leaned over to me and hugged me so tightly I almost stopped breathing.

"I love you," he whispered in my ear.

CHAPTER 5

Hailey shook her head as she stirred sugar sweetener in her iced tea with a knife. She crumbled what looked like fifty little packets and tossed them on the opposite side of the table for the waitress to collect later. I had just given her my post-doctoral visit news.

"I'm sorry to hear that, but tell me the truth; you aren't the least bit relieved?" she asked as she sipped her drink. She reached for another packet, ripped it open and stirred it into her tea. She tasted her concoction once more and nodded to herself, apparently satisfied with the result of the mixture.

"I don't know. I guess a teenie-weenie tiny bit."

"Chile, I would ball up and die, plain and simple. I am not ready for that responsibility. A wailing kid? Uh uh. Not for me."

"Are you serious?" I asked, a bit confused by how adamant she seemed over the thought of being a mother.

"Josephine, please. Could you see me with a brat on my hip? Not happening." She sipped her iced tea and shook her head no rapidly.

"Okay, I get it!" I waited for a moment and told Hailey, "Hmm. Well, Ian and I had the talk."

"*Thee* talk?" Hailey asked while she stretched herself over the table and closer to me to make sure she could hear any interesting tidbits that I was about to say next.

"Yeah. He wants us to get married."

"Oh, snap! Are you excited?"

Clearly Hailey was. I'm sure thoughts of flowers, dresses, groomsmen and catching the bouquet all ran through her mind in that nanosecond.

"Actually, no, I'm not. That's what bothers me."

Hailey leaned backward, apparently disappointed with my declaration, to slump her body against the faux leather bench at our booth. She shook her head slowly from side to side in disbelief for emphasis.

"I think I was more excited about being a mother than getting married," I admitted. "Is that wrong? Because I feel horrible for thinking that way."

"You're asking the wrong person. Have you told him how you feel?"

"Are you crazy? No!"

Hailey shook her head and smirked like she couldn't understand why I wasn't jumping around in my seat, spreading out the latest bridal magazines and discussing possible flavors for the seven-tier cake.

"So what happened after the talk?" she asked with curiosity in her voice.

"What do you think? We had sex."

Hailey tossed her head back and let out a raucous laugh. "Ian is *really* campaigning, huh?"

"Girl, leave Ian alone." I tucked my hand under my chin to keep it propped up. I decided that the conversation regarding me and Ian was about to come to a close. It was time that Hailey told me more about her relationship. Perhaps I should say *relationships*. "Sooo . . . what's up with this mystery man?"

"Not a damn thing and I am *not* gonna talk about him, Josephine, so change the subject," she blared, and then finalized her statement by saying, ". . .with your nosey self!"

"Sorry, but you know I'm bound to find out anyway," I told her flatly. "Besides, I was just going to suggest a girl get-together. It would be nice for my close girl friends to finally meet one another."

Hailey nodded as she looked at me apprehensively. She took a huge gulp of her tea and clanged the glass down on the white butcher paper that covered the wooden tabletop.

"You know I don't like uppity people," she stated plainly.

"My friends aren't uppity. Trust me. Just clear your calendar. I'll have the girls get together first, then we'll do a couples thing since we all are practically hitched."

CHAPTER 6

When Tamar came back to her desk from taking a thirty-minute walk, there was a yellow sticky note on her computer monitor that read *Come See Me* with her new co-worker's signature scribbled underneath.

Her stomach's acrobatic antics made her nauseous before she got up to make the journey to his corner office that should've been hers. She wasn't mentally prepared to deal with a reprimand, but she was prepared to make her feelings known about this corporate double-cross.

Tamar, however, liked the fact that he was all about getting straight down to business and was going to nip any differences in the bud before the work relationship went any further. If the tables were turned and a "subordinate" behaved the way Tamar did with Donovan, she would've pulled them up on it the first chance she had. She may not have been as diplomatic as Donovan appeared he may be. She would've followed the disgruntled co-worker outside of the building and probably would've gotten down to the bottom of their problem right then and there. It wasn't the soundest practice, but the employee would have known that Tamar held her position and job with the highest regard enough to not tolerate any bull from anyone.

Tamar took a deep breath before she started down the corridor to see what Donovan wanted with her. She knew she was in some sort of trouble, but was unsure how he would deliver the news.

Tamar tapped on the door with her fingernail. "You wanted to see me?" she asked in a non-threatening tone. She did not bother to cross the threshold until he indicated it would be okay to do so.

"Yes. Come in, close the door and sit down." Donovan's tone was firm and he kept his eyes on his computer monitor.

She did as instructed. The afternoon walk calmed her down and she realized that her reaction was hardly the welcome that he anticipated. Before she could muster up an apology, he spoke.

"Tamar, I know you're upset. But I am in a position to help. You have to trust me."

"This is the third time I've been passed over for a partnership," Tamar informed him. "What else do I have to do to be a partner around here?"

"I'm glad you asked that question." Donovan rocked back in his chair, lifted his arms, locked his fingers and placed them behind his head. His wrinkle-free, light blue, dress shirt highlighted his muscular arms. He pressed his lips together and stared up to the ceiling in thought.

What a tease and what a damn good looking man. Tamar tried to remember why she was angry and struggled to keep up the momentum, but it was difficult with him sitting there inches away from her looking good enough to hit off right there in that leather, swiveling chair.

"You grab some dinner for yourself and I'll see you tonight back here at seven. Have your thinking cap on because we have a lot of work to do."

"Tonight? At seven? You're joking, right?" she asked.

"No. I'm an easy person to work for, but I didn't appreciate the brush off earlier. I don't play that Miss Thang."

"Excuse me?" Tamar dropped her shoulders while she sat there fighting the temptation to quit on the spot.

Donovan's eyes met hers and the corners of his mouth turned up slightly as he revealed a sly grin that disappeared quickly. He turned his attention back to his monitor to dismiss her. Tamar shook her head and pounded the floor with her feet as she darted back toward her desk, cursing inaudibly along the way.

When seven o'clock arrived, Donovan made his way to Tamar's office where her head lay on the desk as she tried to catch a nap before the after-hours work ensued.

Donovan rapped loudly on her door and asked, "You ready?"

Tamar sprang to attention like a clown in a Jack-In-The-Box and pretended that she wasn't dozing. Without answering, she stood and followed him as he led the way to his office. She couldn't help but to observe his frame from the bottom to the top for the entire stroll. *He probably played football in college*, she thought. *Bowlegs, nice ass, narrow hips and waist, muscular back and broad shoulders: Is it sexual harassment if I imagine tackling him to the floor and forcefully mounting him?*

As Tamar gazed at his exquisite ass, he swung his head around and flashed a warm smile. She looked up quickly and forced a guilty grin. No matter how hard she was checking him out and creating a lustful motion picture of them entwined in her mind, the fact still stood that he was #1 on her blacklist.

When they reached his office he pulled out a chair for her to sit down. Tamar carefully sat down and smoothed her skirt over her thighs. Donovan closed his door and sat down across from her.

"Tamar, I wanted everyone to be gone before talking to you." He loosened his tie and unclasped the top button of his shirt. "I want you to let it out."

"Let it out?"

"Yes, off the record. Tell me how you feel about today. Talk to me as if I were your best friend."

Tamar narrowed her eyes and looked at him suspiciously.

"Go on. I won't hold anything against you." He pressed an index finger to his temple and rested his head there as he waited for her to spew her feelings about the firm's choice to delay announcing partner. "Please, Tamar."

Because Tamar was the type of person that always expressed herself without guilt, this was a piece of cake for her. She hoped he was ready for what she was about to say and that he truly meant that he wouldn't hold anything she said against her later.

"Okay. I think it stinks. I'm *not* thrilled that you're here. I *don't* look forward to working with you and taking your orders. I deserved that partnership, not some *dude* off the street that hasn't put in the hours, gone to the boring social functions, sat through numerous meetings, stayed up late working on briefs, closing arguments and endured months and months of bad potluck dishes from the co-workers here just to get passed over again. If you think for one minute that I'm going to work every night and dissipate *my* social life just so *you* can look good, you are outta your fuckin' mind."

Tamar took a deep breath and sat back in her seat with her arms folded tightly across her chest. Her heart felt light once she had transferred her thoughts that she'd been holding all day onto his virgin ears.

Donovan smiled and then started laughing. "Bad potluck dishes!"

Tamar shook her head in disbelief and waited for him to conclude his chuckling. He rose out of his chair to stand behind Tamar. He placed a comforting hand on her shoulder and gently squeezed. He then slowly leaned closer to whisper in her ear and his lips grazed it softly.

"Doesn't that feel better?"

He straightened up, walked around her and knelt in front of her. Tamar looked deep into his eyes as he caught a glimpse of her cleavage and took in every inch of her long, slender legs.

"I wish you would stay," he said.

"Stay for the firm or for you?"

He stared longingly at her lips before he looked in her eyes to answer her question. "Both," he confessed.

Tamar's eyes focused on his neck before she leaned over to gently bite down on his exposed flesh. Donovan, unable to deny his attraction to Tamar, wrapped his arms around her and planted a hard kiss on her lips.

"I'm gonna tear your ass apart," Tamar declared as she reached down and began massaging his thick manhood that was nestled between his legs.

Donovan placed his hands underneath her skirt and pushed aside her panties with his fingers. His chest heaved up and down rapidly and Tamar gently felt his chest with her fingertips before she ripped his shirt apart. Buttons flew about, clanging against different objects of the room.

She stared at his chest and began licking his nipples, one to the other. She caressed his stomach that felt as hard and rippled as kernels on an ear of corn. His hands cupped her breasts as he squeezed them. Tamar gripped his beltline, unfastened his crocodile skinned-belt and slowly slid it out of the loops of his pants.

They both stood and pressed their bodies tightly against each other. Tamar spun him around by his hips and he looked over his shoulder at her, panting with delight. She folded the belt and gave him a single hard hit on his ass.

"Oh, yes, Tamar! Yes . . ." he moaned.

"That's for taking my job," she whispered in his ear as she spanked his ass again with the belt. Unable to sustain his arousal, he turned around and planted a deep French kiss on her mouth and he raked all of the contents off of his desk. He lay Tamar gently on the hard, flat surface and lifted her skirt up to her waist. With her help, he slid her underwear down to her ankles and removed them. He stuffed her black-laced thong in his pocket and grabbed her legs to slide her down the desktop closer toward him with a single tug.

Tamar rested her feet on his shoulders as he began to lap up every drop of feminine wetness with his tongue. He fluttered his tongue quickly making her dizzy. Her hands blindly reached for something to hold on to as she could feel her body about to explode from the inside out. When Tamar realized that there was nothing within reach, she grabbed her full breasts and squeezed as hard as her delicate hands could.

"Oh, my dear God!" she yelled to the Almighty while releasing her orgasm into Donovan's thirsty mouth. As Tamar lay there trying to gather her senses, Donovan rapidly undressed himself and lifted her off of the table. Her legs felt as strong as two rubber bands that caused her to rest her body against him while he unfastened her skirt. It fell to her ankles and Donovan stood closely behind her. She could feel his bulky, stiffened rod grazing her ass as he led her to the large window that overlooked the city below.

Donovan spread Tamar's legs with his and positioned her ass where he wanted it. She rested the palms of her hands against the glass and peered over her shoulder to watch him enter her. He gripped her plump ass and gave one cheek a firm slap that stung for a few seconds. Tamar's pelvis rippled with anticipation as she reached between her legs to caress his gigantic stick and ball sac. The thickness filled her hand and she smiled to herself. She moved from the perfect position Donovan placed her in so she could see what felt to be a wonderful work of art.

Donovan smiled to mirror Tamar's enthusiasm as he hesitated before unwrapping a condom. Tamar caressed his shaft up and down slowly in her hands. He inhaled deeply and leaned his head back in elation. She knelt down to taste him – she had to.

She slowly slid her tongue up, down, and all around his dick as if it were a delicious piece of candy. As sweet as a long, hardened Sugar Daddy, she began to slowly swallow his penis and sucked it slowly in and out, in and out. With her free hand, she caressed his scrotum and thighs lightly with her fingertips. Donovan ran his fingers through Tamar's hair as he watched her swallow him deeper into her warm, innocent mouth. He began moaning and having spasms as he thrust himself deeper inside her. She sucked harder and faster, trying to fight the urge to drain him dry, because her body anxiously wanted to feel him deep inside of her. As his penis felt harder and larger, she carefully eased his tool from between her lips.

"I want this dick right now!"

"Get that sexy ass back up against that glass so I can work it," he demanded in a throaty tone with his penis erect and parallel to the floor.

Tamar obeyed his instructions and stuck her ass out for him to enter her. *I must be crazy*, she thought to herself. She had never done anything like this before, let alone on the job. But she couldn't help herself. When she first saw Donovan, something ignited within her that sent a tingling sensation through the length of her spine that tickled her clitoris. Something allowed her to give in to her inhibitions and enjoy this man.

Donovan pressed his midsection against Tamar's awaiting ass and then used his fingers to play with her love button. He slid one finger inside and then another.

"Mmmm…" he softly moaned signaling his approval. The sound graced her ears like a note from a cello. She felt his warm hands grip her hips as he entered, and he then whispered, "You are so tight."

Donovan caressed Tamar's back with his fingertips and played with her spine, still savoring the fit. His hands almost completely covered the span of her waist. He continued pumping slowly, in and out, and then more ferociously into her body. Tamar tried to focus on the symphony of colorful lights that danced below from the tenth floor, but she felt lightheaded. She studied the reflection of their intertwined bodies as she felt the imploding pressure of what would be a fierce orgasm.

Tamar's body rippled with chills like a pebble cast into a calm river as she could feel the overflow of her feminine wetness flowing down her inner thighs. Her hands slid down the glass as she reached around to grip his firm ass to push him deeper inside of her. He didn't allow her to come down from her orgasmic high before he started stroking her harder and faster. Surrendering, she placed her palms on the glass and leaned forward preparing for the next orgasm, and the next, and yet another.

Donovan unlocked his grasp from Tamar's waist and slid his hands up her back and around to her breasts. She felt his strong hands squeeze them in the same rhythm of his long, deep strokes. He was pushing himself deeper inside of her, bucking like a wild stallion to reach his climax. She could feel a wave of electric currents in her lower abdomen that would prepare her to answer his hard, maniacal stroking with a thunder of orgasms.

"Hmm, yeah, baby. I feel that," Donovan moaned, sucking in air through his clenched teeth as he stroked faster and faster until he climaxed and pulled her hips down onto him. He took a moment to gather his senses and catch his breath. He then pulled her up and twisted her around slightly to kiss him over her shoulder.

"Oh my God," Donovan confessed, his hands still resting on Tamar's hips. "You drive me crazy, baby."

Tamar gazed over at his desk clock that sat atop a cardboard box labeled *Office*. The clock read eleven thirty. *So much for leaving at nine*, she chuckled to herself. Donovan turned her to face him and began kissing her all over. Her hands rested on his edible shoulders as he knelt down to hug her hips and kiss her stomach. She arched her back as she felt the hot tip of his tongue circle her bellybutton. He rose to give her another passionate kiss as he squeezed her close to him.

Quitting the job now was the farthest thing from her mind.

CHAPTER 7

Camilla decided to do some "campaigning" of her own to gain the total interest of Bryan Bryant. Bryan was returning from Detroit after hosting one of his book signings and Camilla thought it would be the perfect time to surprise him with a romantic candlelight dinner and some good loving afterward.

From what Camilla told me, she picked up a few tips from some Kama Sutra book that she borrowed from the library. I had no idea that the library would carry such items, but on the other hand, it *is* a library. Camilla showed me the book and I perused a few of its pages and made mental notes on a few positions that I wouldn't mind trying out with Ian. When I thumbed through to about the tenth page or so, Camilla grabbed the book from me and told me that I needed to find one of my own. She was so engrossed in that book the entire time that Bryan was away in Detroit that she debated keeping the book for herself instead of returning it. When I asked her why she didn't just buy one, her solution to her small dilemma hit her in that instant.

"I'll just take it to work and copy it!"

By the time Bryan got to Camilla's house, he was almost an hour late and offered no explanation. An hour late was an improvement. The first month of their "relationship" he wouldn't even call to tell her he was running late. Usually, she had to call to make sure he was still on his way, or just sit and wait. Camilla decided again to let his tardiness slide and to focus on gaining his attention and affection for the rest of the night.

"How about some wine?" Camilla asked him as she presented an aged bottle of fine red wine.

"No, thank you. I have an article due tomorrow afternoon and need to keep my head right."

Bryan flopped down on her couch and looked around at her trinkets and furniture dispassionately as if he were in a showroom at Ikea.

"Don't sit there! I made us dinner," she tugged at his arm.

He stiffened at her touch. "Camilla, I ate after I got off of the plane," he said as he pulled his hand back from her and pressed out the front of his pants with the palms of his hands.

She looked down at the floor as she stood in front of him. "I was just trying to give you a surprise."

Bryan realized his rudeness and her attempt to woo him and reached for her hand. "I'm sorry, Camilla. It's a very nice surprise. Why don't you wrap everything up and we can eat it tomorrow after I send in my article?"

"You mean it? You're coming over again tomorrow?"

"Yes," he smiled as he looked at her and it forced Camilla to smile as well.

"Okay, I'll do that then." She happily flopped down beside him on the couch and snuggled up next to him. "So what do you want to do then since dinner is off of the itinerary?"

Bryan smiled to himself and then looked back at her. He leaned over and whispered in her ear.

Camilla's mouth slowly turned upward into a smile and she lightly punched him in the arm. "You are *so* nasty!"

Bryan began kissing her neck and slid his tongue in her ear. Camilla rolled her eyes around in pleasure and began caressing his inner thigh.

She mumbled to him, "It's a good thing that I'm nasty too."

With that affirmation, Bryan picked Camilla up and headed toward her bedroom. This is what he came over for. Not dinner or aged wine, just Camilla. He carefully placed her on the bed and began to undress her delicately. Camilla was reviewing all of the Kama Sutra positions that she had crammed into her brain the two days that Bryan was gone. Tonight, with her feminine wiles and newfound sexual expertise, she was determined to ignite something within Bryan that would bring her one step closer to monogamy with him.

Unfortunately for Camilla, tonight was *not* going to be the night.

Bryan offered her two, maybe three minutes of foreplay before he began stroking himself inside of her. He didn't even look at her while he was on top of her. Instead he focused on her headboard and looked over at the window a few times.

The room was dark with the exception of the moonlight coming in the window and the glow of the chandelier from the dining room.

Camilla pulled herself up to him to be kissed. He gave her a quick peck on the lips and forced his torso on top of her to keep her down. He placed his chin over her right shoulder and buried his face in her pillow as his strokes became more rapid.

Soon, it would be over, much to Camilla's dissatisfaction. She did not get the opportunity to experiment with the positions she learned in the book. These were positions that she learned just to be used on Bryan. She wanted to feel that closeness that she longed for, but Bryan kept his emotional distance from her.

Bryan made little noise when he came ten minutes after he started. He breathed heavily, let out a small moan and rolled over on his back to catch his breath.

Camilla sat up and began to caress his chest and kiss it gently. Bryan looked up at the ceiling, still heaving as his body glistened with perspiration. He licked his lips and moistened his throat by swallowing hard. He rubbed Camilla's shoulder and sat up.

"Let me take this condom off, baby."

Bryan made his way to the bathroom. When he flicked on the light, it nearly blinded Camilla causing her to squint. He closed the door gently and Camilla heard the running water from the faucet.

"Shit," she said under her breath.

She flopped back on the bed and stared up at the ceiling. Not long after, the sound of the shower disrupted her thoughts of an unfulfilled orgasm yet again. She thought that maybe he was stressed out from the plane ride or had too much on his plate at the moment. Camilla told herself that once Bryan gets his next book completed, he will be focused and all about her.

Until that day came, Camilla reached over and opened the top drawer to her nightstand. She fished around for her butterfly toy and propped her legs up on the bed as if she were about to be examined. She rubbed the tips of her fingers over her moistened vulva and placed the toy in position. With one flick of the switch, she would get the deserved pleasure that Bryan Bryant failed to deliver. Sure, it was nice to feel the weight of him pressed firmly against her body along with his kisses, but she wanted to explode from the inside out and Bryan Bryant, with all of his newfound fame, books and busy schedule was not up to the task.

By the time the shower was turned off, Camilla had reached her climax, tucked the toy back in the nightstand and fell off into a light sleep.

Bryan stepped out of the bathroom, looked at Camilla's angelic face while she slept, grinned to himself and began to get dressed.

He tiptoed into her kitchen and made as little noise as possible while he fished around her cabinets for a few Tupperware bowls and lids. He cracked open her aged wine and poured him a large glass. After he swallowed that down, he thought it would be a shame to waste it, so he decided to take the bottle along with him. He also packed himself a doggie bag of the meal she spent hours preparing.

Once his mission was complete, he silently left.

CHAPTER 8

Tamar and Donovan were free to see each other without the threat of being part of any office gossip. The day after their romp in his corner office, Tamar came into work as normal, with the exception of using public transportation. She opted to drive in to the office. She spoke to the security guard at the front desk like she often did and entertained him with small talk while she waited in the lobby for the elevator. She walked into the law office where she worked loyally for four years on the 10th floor, exchanged pleasantries with the receptionists and unlocked her office door.

She opened her calendar on her computer and cleared all of her activities for the day. She also erased the messages from her voicemail without listening to any of them. Donovan walked by her office and doubled back when he saw that she was at her desk. He lightly tapped on the door. Tamar looked up and, when she noticed it was Donovan, she smiled ever so slightly. He returned her smile with a silent blow of a kiss.

"I'll stop by in a few," she informed him.

"Great," he smiled. "I'll make sure there aren't any meetings scheduled so we can . . . uhh . . . talk."

They smiled again at each other, both sharing a secret that no one else in the office knew. Donovan left and Tamar continued going through some of her semi-personal files that she stored on the company's computer. One file that she was looking for in particular, she wrote yesterday and saved it just before she met privately with Donovan. She printed that file to the printer that was located on her desk. Once the paper slowly scrolled out of the machine, Tamar reached for it, grabbed her black pen and scribbled on it.

Tamar shut the electrical equipment off and started toward Donovan's office.

"Hey," she said once she got to his office. She no longer felt the need to knock before she entered, or wait at the threshold of his office before being allowed entry. They were well past those formalities.

"Hello there," he swiveled his chair in her direction and ceased working. "I'm glad you dropped by."

"Here," she said and handed him the folded piece of paper.

"What's this, babe?" He took the paper from her and opened it. He read the first sentence and stopped himself from reading any further. "Tamar, don't do this, baby."

"I have to, Donovan."

"I know you may not think so, but I *can* help you."

"I can't take that chance, Donovan," she said sympathetically. "I'm sorry. We've seen each other naked and were all over this office last night. I can't."

Although the sex was incredible and working together would've been somewhat awkward, Donovan still tried to get her to reconsider leaving the job. For Tamar, working there was no longer an option. She never had sex before with a co-worker, boss or even a janitor that worked in the same building for that matter, and she was not about to start now.

This was safer for her.

"I understand, Tamar," he said with a burdened expression. He tossed the resignation letter on his desktop and caressed his mouth and down to his chin in thought. "Yeah," he started, "I understand, but you aren't getting away from me that easily. I want to see you again. And again, and again."

After Tamar left the law firm that day, she and Donovan saw each other almost every evening over the next three weeks. They went out to eat, went on mini-road trips and even took in a few of the many historic venues of DC. They discovered different things about each other in and out of the bedroom. Tamar sensed that Donovan wanted to get a little closer, but she wasn't prepared for that at all. Not that she wanted to sleep with other men, because she enjoyed the sex with Donovan. She just didn't want to get wrapped up in some whirlwind romance in just three weeks.

Each time Donovan tried, she pumped the brakes and put things in perspective for the both of them. He made a personal commitment to help her find a new job. She was appreciative of his efforts, but wanted to do it for herself.

Tamar was the type of woman that took the word "independent" to a whole new level. She didn't want handouts or sympathy and preferred that people were upfront with her no matter how harsh it may seem.

When she was growing up, her mother often told her that she would never sugarcoat anything for Tamar's benefit because the world would not afford her that luxury. That bit of her mother's advice was something that Tamar kept with her for all of those years. Because of that, Tamar developed a sixth sense and knew when someone was bullshitting her.

"I have a case to prepare for, baby," Donovan told her. "Do you want to help me?"

"No," Tamar stated plainly as she continued flipping through the want ads.

"What's wrong, Tamar? Are you still upset about not getting that promotion? It's been three weeks. Relax. Everything is going to work out for you."

"Donovan, honey, I know how long it's been. And, no, I'm not mad at you. I'm mad at myself, but I'll be fine. I had a few calls today. I'll be fine."

"I'm telling you, I know this lady that can hook you up with a six-figure gig Downtown at this law firm. She's in the position to do it for you, baby."

Tamar huffed and folded up the paper before tossing it on the coffee table. "Donovan, I told you, I appreciate it, but . . . I got this." She patted his thigh and stood up to go toward the kitchen.

Donovan jumped up and blocked her retreat. He stood in front of her and looked down at her brandishing a sly grin. He caressed his midsection against her and bent over to kiss her neck.

Tamar, obviously impressed with his eagerness to please her, smiled to herself and kissed him square on his mouth as she massaged the back of his neck.

"Do your work," she commanded.

Her hand brushed his stomach and down to his groin as she walked into the kitchen. His hungry eyes followed her and struggled to suppress the heat that rose in his loins. He flopped down on the couch and grabbed his leather portfolio and stack of files.

"Do you want something to eat?" she called out.

"You," he called back to her.

"Chill, dude. Do your work." She giggled to herself. "Hey, I need to run an errand. I'll be back in a bit, okay?"

Donovan looked up from his stack of work and in Tamar's direction. His eyebrows were furrowed as he began to be overcome with concern.

"Where you going?"

"To run some errands. I'll be back, sweetie."

Tamar stood in front of him and leaned over to kiss him. She caressed his cheek and gave him a second kiss.

"Don't be long. I'll be done with this in no time. I got something I want to give to you." He winked at her and placed his hand on the small of her back and pulled her gently toward him.

"I bet you do." She blew him a kiss and left.

When Tamar got into her car, she rested the back of her head on the headrest for a moment before turning the ignition. She sighed and pressed her eyes shut as tight as she could.

"What have I done?" she said aloud.

She started the car and wheeled out of Donovan's driveway.

CHAPTER 9

Ian had to be the best guy in the whole world. Even though I keep telling him that I was okay about not being pregnant, he has been overly attentive and acting as though I was about seven months into term.

When I told him that I was going to have my friends get together to meet one another, he did not get all insecure like some of the guys I've had in the past. He even offered to cook for my little shindig. And as much as I enjoy his culinary skills, he is my best-kept secret and to put it plainly, "he's all mine."

I stocked up at a local Price Club and that was the extent of the preparation. Silently throughout the store, I prayed that all of the girls would get along. Even though I understood them and they understood me, understanding each other was a totally different story.

Camilla wanted to bring movies from her collection of "The World Just Doesn't Understand Me" greatest hits, but I politely talked her out of it. The idea was for us to get to know one another. I thought since it was just the four of us, it shouldn't be a difficult task.

Ian and Hailey's boyfriend, Steve, were going to hang out while the girls were scoffing down food and drinking white wine by the box full.

We were all standing around in the kitchen nibbling on the different types of finger food and sipping on wine and margaritas.

"So are we gonna watch one of those chick flicks?" Hailey asked.

"No," Camilla chimed in. "I was talked out of bringing them."

"You let Josephine stop you from bringing *your* movies?" Hailey scoffed. "You should've brought them anyway, girlfriend. I can't believe you let little ol' Josephine punk you."

"Camilla," I interrupted, "I have all of your old, cheesy movies anyway. I was just saving you some trouble, but I see how you roll. Actually," I said as I pointed from Camilla to Hailey, "I see how you *both* roll."

"Well, what do you have, Josie?" Tamar asked with a chuckle. She was the only one that called me Josie, other than some of my co-workers.

"Okay, well, what mood are we in today?" Hailey asked. "There is an art to picking out the perfect video, you know?"

Tamar stopped sipping her wine and stared at Hailey for a moment.

"I know that sounded a bit pathetic," Hailey started, "but work with a sista!"

They both laughed as Tamar poured more wine into Hailey's glass. Camilla chucked a teriyaki-glazed meatball in her mouth and looked around at the other finger food that she may have had a taste for at the moment.

"So what are you guys in the mood for," I asked them. "Something funny, something girly, some action, suspense? What?"

"How 'bout 'I want him, but just not *all* the time?'" Tamar said as she emptied her plate into the trash.

"*Runaway Bride*," Hailey blurted out as if she were on a game show about to win a prize for her efforts.

"Uh oh," I chimed in. "I know you're not talking about Donovan?"

At that question, Hailey and Camilla perked up. I'm sure they were thinking, *Finally, some dirt!*

"Girl, yes!" Tamar placed both hands on her head as if she were thwarting off an oncoming migraine. "I mean, don't get me wrong, I enjoy him, but he is just trying to put the handcuffs on a sista. Is the phrase '*I need to breathe*' in his vocabulary?"

"Well, at least yours wants to be chained to a sista," Camilla pointed out. "Mine, oh, if I can even call him *mine*, is doing everything possible to make it a point that he is not about to be put on lockdown."

"What about you, Hailey?" Tamar asked her.

"We are just enjoying each other," she replied in a way as to prevent giving away too many details.

"Yeah, for *fifty* years!" I exaggerated with a scoff. "You guys could've been married, divorced, widowed and having a séance with each other as long as y'all have been *enjoying* each other."

"That ain't even right, Josephine," Hailey defended. "You and Ian have been riding the wave for a minute too now."

"I know, but we have had *the talk.*"

I poured myself another glass of wine and brought the bottle into the living room. The other ladies followed with their glasses and got comfortable on the furniture. I set the bottle down in the middle of the coffee table and stretched out on the sofa, putting my feet on Hailey who sat at the opposite end.

"You and your dogs!" Hailey frowned when she looked at my socked feet as I chuckled.

"So, what's going on with Donovan?" I asked.

"Well, dude is getting strung out. Like the other day, I made up a lie about having to run errands just to get away from him. He said he had work to do and since he stole my job, I would hate for him to get fired. Then my resignation would've been in vain."

"He stole your job?" Camilla asked.

"Not really. My boss double-crossed me and gave the promotion that I rightfully deserved to an outsider. That outsider just happened to be Donovan. Well, I wasn't having it, so I quit and now Donovan wants me to come back to the firm, which won't be happening."

"And you thought *you* had drama," I looked at Hailey when I said that.

"What's your story?" Tamar asked Hailey.

"Okay, Steve and I have been dating for a while. Neither of us has mentioned marriage. Not that I don't want to, but I'm not pressing it. So while he's making up his mind, I've been getting me some beefcake from someone else."

"Oh, my God!" Camilla yelled.

"And it's good too!" Hailey concluded and slapped me a high-five.

"You know, the other night, me and my friend were together, he can not do it at all," Camilla confessed. "I may have to get me some beefcake too."

We laughed at her plight.

"He just stares at the headboard or looks out of the window. What's up with that?" Camilla asked us.

"Girl, he's thinking about someone else," Tamar told her bluntly.

"What?" Camilla could barely believe her ears. Tamar, who was almost a stranger, told her flat out what was going through Bryan Bryant's mind.

"It's a dead giveaway. Now when they are pumping on you like there is no tomorrow, you are turning them on and they literally cannot control themselves. Trust me, I know."

"I know you know," I co-signed her statement and she winked at me.

"That bastard," Camilla said. "You know he had the nerve to make himself a doggie-bag before he left my house. Took my good bottle of wine. No, poured himself a glass, left it dirty in my sink, *then* took the bottle! We were supposed to save that food and wine for the next day!"

Almost in unison, we all laughed. Camilla, not understanding our laughter, looked at us for a moment before she joined in with us.

"Did he call or come by the next day? No!" she finalized. "What a jerk."

"All men want is some good puss and some good food," Tamar told us.

*   *   *   *

By the time Hailey got home from the get together, Steve wasn't too far behind her. Whatever he and Ian did that night to occupy their time was not her concern. But she was concerned that Steve was too exhausted when she tried to initiate sex with him.

"Come on, baby," Hailey pleaded as she kissed and licked on his neck.

Steve gave a pleasurable moan, but turned away from her slightly. Hailey, not used to the brush off, felt a bit rejected, but recuperated from her bruised ego quickly. She wasn't completely offended by the dismissal from Steve because she had already made it up in her mind to hook up with her mystery man the next day.

Steve gave her an apologetic look and took off his Timberland boots. "Sorry, babe," he quietly offered.

"So what'd you guys do? Strip club?" she asked jokingly, already knowing the answer.

"Something like that."

"That's why no sex tonight?"

"No baby. I'm tired. It's two in the morning. But I *am* a little hungry though. Can you fix me a sandwich?"

Hailey tossed her coat in the closet without putting it on a hanger. She turned and looked at Steve with an offensive glare before she scoffed and walked into the bedroom.

Steve shook his head and walked toward the kitchen. Instead of making himself a sandwich, he grabbed a cereal bar, ripped the paper off of it and began munching. By the time he made it to the bedroom where Hailey was undressing, he had finished the snack and peeled off his shirt. He hopped on the bed and flicked on the TV.

"Turn that off," she commanded.

"Why? I want to see some TV."

"You're *tired*, remember? Turn it off please." Hailey flicked the light switch off and climbed in the bed.

Steve looked over at her as she prepared for slumber; her eyes already closed tight. He exhaled as loud as he could as he lay on his back and stared up at the ceiling. After a few moments, his eyes began to adjust to the dark and he looked over at his girlfriend who appeared to be sleeping. Her shoulder was exposed and he lightly caressed it. She didn't move.

Steve flipped over on his side to spoon and began gently kissing her shoulder. He caressed her back and ran his hand down the length of her body. When he rubbed his hand across her hip, he rested it in the slope of her waist. He gave a gentle squeeze and she turned around to face him.

"Don't be mad," he told her in between kisses.

Hailey gave him several pecks on the lips and both of his cheeks. She caressed his chest and rose up on her side to suck on his neck tenderly.

Steve began to disappear.

His body had shrunk lower and lower beneath the sheets until he was face to face with her midsection. Hailey looked down at the lump in her bed as it maneuvered itself under the covers to find her treasure. When it was discovered, she threw her head back revealing the full length of her neck and let out a soft moan. She lifted both arms up over her head and gripped the rails of the headboard. She did not let go of the headboard as he ferociously stimulated her. She gyrated her hips in a circular motion as she met his thirsty mouth and lapping tongue. She didn't let go of the rails from the headboard until she came. She slowly loosened her grip as if the aftershocks depended on it.

"Damn, baby!" she said behind a satisfied and heavy sigh.

Out of breath, she stayed in her orgasmic position for about three minutes as she enjoyed her descent from cloud nine. One thing that Hailey was sure of was Steve was the best guy to ever please her orally.

At that moment, Hailey wanted nothing more than to make Steve that sandwich that he asked for earlier. Unfortunately for him, right now she could not assemble enough strength to make the journey into the kitchen, let alone handle utensils and deli ham and cheese. *It will have to wait until morning,* she thought to herself.

"I'll make you breakfast," she whispered to Steve just before she fell off into a heavy sleep.

CHAPTER 10

Camilla felt powerless. All of her efforts to seduce Bryan Bryant and make him her own were foiled. Her sex wasn't sustaining him, even though she did not experience more than five minutes of pleasure from him, and her thoughtfulness and supportive nature fell by the wayside. Nothing seemed to work. Camilla had no clue how to win this man over. She knew he enjoyed her cooking because that seemed to be the one thing he would come over for, followed by him obtaining a "quickie" from her. Bryan definitely enjoyed her bottle of red wine and had an affinity for her Tupperware. It was a large pill to swallow, but Camilla came to realize that Bryan just did not like her. She would have to end things with him permanently. Unfortunately, getting her Tupperware back from him would be a separate feat.

Reluctantly, she pulled herself out of her car and began to walk down the sidewalk toward the three-story building of the local library. She took one last look at the Kama Sutra book, caressed it lovingly as if it were the Holy Grail and dumped it into the drop box. Her shoulders lifted and dropped with the accompaniment of a loud and heavy exhalation.

Camilla turned toward her car and decided to grab the *City Paper* and go to a nearby coffee shop to see what events she could crash this upcoming weekend. She figured that she may as well go out and make herself available again. She wasn't the type of person who enjoyed being alone for weeks at a time. While she longed for a loving relationship, she felt she had little control over who came her way. Through her desperation, she entertained the likes of some men who seldom met her criteria, all for the hope of him possibly turning into "the one." It was a shallow but whirling eddy of degradation, but she was determined to be engaged by 30 — or so she hoped.

When she arrived to the coffee house, strangely it wasn't as crowded as normal. She thought to herself, *Great! I can read in peace.* She ordered her Grande Café Latte and found a nice table tucked near the rear of the shop, but still visible.

It was not until she got about midway through her latte that she noticed a nice gentleman sitting at a table just opposite of hers. He was tall and lanky, but cute. He had the most adorable, boyish eyes that she had seen on a grown man. Instinctively, she noticed his hands and thought to herself, *Good! No ring.* She watched him as he read his copy of the *City Paper.* She thought that this was fate. They were reading the same paper and they both were probably looking for something to do this weekend. This was her segue to an introduction.

Immediately, she liked him and wondered what she could say to him that would spark his interest enough to want to spend some time with her.

Throwing all caution to the wind, she walked over to his table and stood in front of him. When he realized that she was doing more than just waiting to pass, but waiting to speak to him, he looked up and gave her a warm smile.

His smile lit up Camilla's world. Although she had no idea who this man was, she felt an instant connection and warmth from him. His friendly smile was comforting and she wanted to know more about the man behind it. She wondered if perhaps someday she would find use for those Kama Sutra positions after all.

"Hi, I'm sorry to bother you," she started. "You look so engrossed."

"Oh, that's okay," he said as he set the paper down on the tabletop and waited for her to continue. He looked her up and down and was pleased with what he saw.

"I was just reading the same paper and wondered if you were able to find anything interesting to do this weekend? I couldn't." She frowned and held up the paper to prove that this was a come on line with props.

"Oh. Uh, I wasn't really checking for that. It's just something to read when I don't feel like reading *The Post.* It seems like every article in there is damn near written by Bryan Bryant," he chuckled as he took a swig of his coffee.

Camilla felt a slight twinge in her stomach as Bryan's name was mentioned. This guy couldn't possibly know that she dated him, could he? Besides, her and Bryan rarely went anywhere in public. At least nowhere the common DC'er would venture to.

"Tell me all about it. My name is Camilla." She extended her hand for him to shake.

"That's a very pretty name, Camilla. I like it. My name is Steve."

"So I would enjoy some company to one of these places this weekend. Are you up for it?"

"Wow. That would be nice, but I'm sort of involved with someone."

As Camilla stood over him, she looked slightly disappointed but refused to throw in the towel so easily. She wanted to prove to herself that she was still desirable despite the way that Bryan made her feel. To her, if this guy rejected her, it would be a devastating blow to her ego. Sure, different men liked different types of women, but she craved this affirmation from Steve since she was immediately drawn to him.

"Are you guys married?"

"No."

"Engaged?"

"No," he said with a light chuckle.

"Well, you sound like you're single, just not dating. One date couldn't hurt, could it? Then *you* decide if you want a second."

Steve, obviously flattered by her persistence, smiled and blushed as he tried to think of a way to let her down. He was definitely attracted to her. He found her aggressive nature attractive and her petite frame did not hurt her either. When he couldn't think of a nice putdown, he decided not to at all.

"Well, when you put it that way, I guess you're right. One date couldn't hurt."

"Cool!" Camilla said as she reached in her purse and handed him her card. "Are you familiar with Kama Sutra?"

He laughed as he took her card and looked it over.

"Uh, yeah. I've heard of it."

"Oh, well I know it. All I need is a willing subject. It would be a waste for all of that knowledge to go down the drain, Steve."

Steve no longer blushed at her comments. Instead, he looked at her with hunger as he wondered what she would do to him sexually. He eyed her with a plan of what he would do to please himself sexually with her. Steve had a ton of tricks in his goody bag and he surely could entertain an eager participant. Even though Steve was lanky, he was strong and muscular. Camilla seemed so small in size to him, he figured that he could probably pick Camilla up over his head if the evening called for it. Next he felt her place her hand on his shoulder as she gently squeezed.

"Call me," she said.

CHAPTER 11

I called Hailey to see if she wanted to hang out for happy hour after work, but I couldn't reach the bum. She probably had a date planned with her mystery man again. Since I couldn't reach Hailey, I decided to call Ian, who I was able to catch just before he left work for the day. Since I wasn't pregnant, it was back to drinking liquor and eating junk food, and this was the Friday that I wanted to indulge.

Ian agreed to meet me at the jazz club for drinks. It had been a while since Ian and I had gone out, but at least we were not strangers to the idea. He knew I loved live music and anything that concerned the cultural arts. He loved going to sporting events, so we had balance in our relationship, I felt.

When I walked inside, the place was so dim that I could barely see my hand in front of my face. I sat in the bar area that had the most light in the establishment and looked out at the crowd. Maybe it was just me, but the crowd seemed to get younger and younger. I refused to believe I was getting older because I just didn't feel older.

This young guy approached me and wanted to strike up a conversation. If I had to guess, he was probably a senior at Howard or some other surrounding institution of higher learning. He had short, thin dreadlocks with an adorable smile.

"How are you?" he asked, leaning his face toward mine.

"Good. You?" I backed away just a tad.

"Fine. Can I buy you a drink?"

"If you'd like, but I am waiting on someone." I looked toward the door hoping Ian wasn't crossing the room as we spoke.

"A female friend?" he asked with a smile.

I gave him a sympathetic smile and shook my head.

"Oh, your man?"

I nodded. "But you can still buy me a drink if you'd like," I giggled knowing that he was probably thinking to himself that I should get my man to buy me a drink. My hunch was right, but his reply was much too clever for someone who looked to be about 23.

"Oh, is your man broke?" he sort of rolled his eyes when he said that and I got a tad bit offended.

"Hey, don't get angry with me. You approached me. At least I'm being honest."

He smirked and looked me over from head to toe before he forced himself to smile. "You right, sis. I hope he treats you well."

I nodded and placed my hand over my heart. "Oh so right. It was nice meeting you."

The youngster nodded with a smile and walked away to find another woman to buy a drink for. Just as I gave him his walking papers, Ian came over to me and planted a kiss on my mouth.

"Hey, baby. Who was that scrub?"

"No one. He wanted to buy me a drink, but decided it was your job." I placed my hand on his shoulder and rubbed it. "How was your day?"

"I'm glad it's over," he said as he turned to the bartender. "Yo? My man? Give me a beer and get her a B52." He turned back toward me and said, "Mmm, I missed you today. Let's not plan to stay too long. I want to tap that tonight. I may be up for four rounds." He smiled as he looked down my shirt and nibbled on my earlobe.

"Four? Damn, why'd you order the drinks?" I laughed. "As far as I'm concerned, we can roll after you finish your beer. I've been feeling a little frisky today myself." I caressed Ian's face and leaned in to kiss him. I hugged him and rested my chin on his shoulder as he caressed the small of my back.

As I was being hypnotized by his touch, I just happened to look toward the rear of the club and saw Camilla. I couldn't see the guy that she was with because his back was to me, but for some reason he seemed familiar. I snapped out of the trance Ian had placed me under as I jolted my back into an erect position.

"Oh, baby, there's Camilla. Let me go say hi."

"Okay, baby."

As I made my way over to Camilla, the guy left and walked in the direction of where the restrooms were. I tried to see who he was, but with the dim lighting in the club and the guy's unconscious stubbornness to do a 180 so I could see him made it impossible.

"Camilla? Hey!"

Camilla sort of jumped in her seat when she saw me, but got up to hug me. "Hey, girl!"

"What's up? I'm here with Ian." I probed her slightly to see if she would give up information about who she was talking to. Unfortunately, she didn't bite.

"Oh, cool. How is he?" She looked around to try and spot him.

"Good. He's at the bar. So who was that guy?"

"Oh, I met him at the coffeehouse earlier this week. I was so damn persistent and was not about to let him turn me down. I have never done anything like that before. He told me he had a girl, but I was like, 'And? Are you guys married?' So we decided to hang out. Little does he know, I will be laying it on him tonight, girl. He is so damn cute!"

"Do you know this guy?"

"I mean, not really, but I don't care anymore."

I shook my head at Camilla's nonchalant attitude. "Camilla, this dude could be a serial rapist! What do you mean, you don't care?"

"Look, Josephine, there are three knives placed strategically around my bed. I'm not worried about that. Besides, I didn't get that vibe from him at all. You know how your instincts kick into gear if something isn't right? I feel okay with him"

I refused to agree with Camilla's logic on this one, so I just shrugged.

"Well, I didn't feel that way," she said and sipped her frothy-looking beverage that had slices of fruit sticking out of it. "I'm gonna have some fun and try to forget Bryan Bryant. Do you know I called him and asked for my Tupperware and he hasn't called me back yet? With all that money he's supposed to be making, you'd think he could just buy himself some."

Ian brought my drink over to me as I was trying to wait for Camilla's friend to come back.

"I'm done with my beer," he told me with a smile as he placed his hand on the small of my back.

"Hey, baby. You remember Camilla, don't you?"

Camilla smiled and waved her hand at Ian.

"Hey," Ian said. He jiggled my drink in front of me. "Drink up. Nice seeing you again, Camilla, but Josephine promised that we wouldn't be staying long. We gotta roll." He winked at her.

"Oh, I got you. I don't think I'll be staying long either." She lifted her tropical drink up and winked back at him. "I'll holla at you, Josephine!"

Ian carted me back to the bar by my waist as I waved goodbye to Camilla over my shoulder. Instead of guzzling my drink down like I normally would at the idea of getting four rounds of sex from Ian, I sipped my B52 in a desperate attempt to wait out Camilla's man.

When I was about halfway done with my drink, the guy who was sluggish about returning to Camilla's side finally came back. I watched intently, telepathically begging this dude to turn toward me so I could record a mental image of his face. Surprisingly, my psychic skills that I've never been known to possess actually worked! The guy turned almost completely around which afforded me a full frontal of his face.

I damn near dropped my drink to the floor as I gasped. Even Ian reacted to my gesture strangely.

"What's wrong, baby?"

"Oh, God. Camilla is here with Steve."

"Steve who?"

"Your friend! Hailey's Steve!"

Ian tried to turn his head, but I wouldn't let him. Instead, I placed my hand under his chin and kept his face turned in my direction.

"Don't!"

"What?" he tried to turn again, but I stopped him.

"Ian? No. I have to do something."

"I'll tell you what you do, baby. Finish that drink so I can . . ." he whispered in my ear the rest of his statement before he nibbled on it. I blushed and looked around sheepishly as if everyone just heard what he said. My pelvis rippled with anticipation, but I had to thwart off the feeling for just a few more minutes.

"Ian, they are my friends. I can't let this happen."

"Mind your business. Steve wouldn't be here if everything with him and Hailey were all good."

"No, but you don't understand—"

"Josephine, baby, I '*over*stand,' okay? Trust me, don't get in it." Ian took my drink from me and set it on the bar. "Let's roll, baby." He lifted me up from the barstool and tugged me toward the exit.

I looked over at Camilla and Steve who didn't see us leave. They looked engaged in each other. They giggled and flirted, even Steve caressed her chin at one point causing Camilla to blush.

I think Ian meant well, but it was going to be difficult to keep silent. I couldn't very well tell Ian that not only was Steve here with my friend Camilla, Hailey was also cheating on Steve with some mystery man. However, both Hailey and Camilla were my friends. They met each other and hit it off. I even think they exchanged numbers to hang out every now and then. I'm sure that if Camilla knew Steve was Hailey's man, she wouldn't be planning on screwing Steve tonight like she told me. Camilla wouldn't even have approached him if she knew. She may be on a mission, but she would not cross those lines.

Aside from that, the thing that really surprised me was that Steve actually went out with Camilla! According to Camilla, Steve told her that he was in a relationship. I'm unsure what level of detail he provided her about the intricacies of that relationship, but why did Camilla's persistence weaken Steve? Was this a first for him?

This was much too complicated and so far Ian's advice was the best to follow at this point. I was already slightly troubled over the possibility of Camilla and Steve having sex tonight and certainly did not want that image in my head. Ian and I hadn't even made it to the car yet and I had no idea what to do.

What should I do?

CHAPTER 12

Saturday morning, Ian got up to go jogging while I stayed in the bed trying to get the feeling to come back in my legs. Ian wore me out last night. He predicted four rounds and his prediction came to fruition. We hadn't had sex in about six days because of this pregnancy business and Ian delivered sheer intensity and passion in each thrust. I couldn't let him go that long without sex again.

My body yearned for a shower, but I seriously could not move. Every time I closed my eyes, I caught flashbacks of him staring hungrily at my body. Each time I closed my eyes, I felt his fingertips caress my skin as if he were still in the bed with me. Just thinking about our intimacy and lovemaking from the night before almost sent me into a frenzy of orgasms.

I wanted to reach for the phone when it rang, but again, I couldn't move. It rang five times before voicemail picked it up. It was times like these that I wished I had the old-fashioned answering machine where I could hear the person leaving a message. If I wanted to speak to them, I could interrupt them and talk or just let it play on and return the call later. Unfortunately, I would have to grab the phone, dial a special number to access voicemail, and then punch in my access code to hear the message. And right now, I was not going to attempt to move.

I stared at the ceiling and rubbed my hands across my body as I imagined that they were Ian's. I smiled to myself. Every muscle in my body was exhausted and that meant that later today they would all stiffen and become sore.

Last night, Ian actually flipped me upside down as the tops of my thighs rested on his shoulders while we both feasted. I sucked on him as if he were a delicious caramel flavored lollipop. This position caused all of the blood to rush to my head. Before I felt my sugar walls about to detonate, I pleaded with him to flip me right side up, which he ignored. He was enjoying having his dick sucked.

"Ian, please! No, no, no!"

"Umm hmm," he knowingly murmured as he continued devouring my silken folds.

"Oh, no . . . oh, shi- . . . Ian! I said no! Ooooooooo wooooo!!!" After the initial yell, I began whimpering like a wounded pup as my pulsating thighs tightened around his neck. When I had my orgasm in that position and screamed as loudly as I had, that made my head hurt temporarily.

Carefully, and with the headache now in full effect this morning, I lifted my body up and reached for the phone. I checked the waiting message and it was Hailey.

"Girl, you won't believe this. Steve did not come home last night. Call me back."

My eyes opened wide as I slammed the phone into the receiver. With energy that must have been on reserve, I sprang up and ran to the bathroom to hop in the shower. My intention would be to leave Ian a note and be out of the house before he came back.

For the entire time that I was in the shower attempting to wash away the soreness from last night I could hear Ian's voice. Even as I sprung a few curls in my hair, I continued to hear Ian's voice inside my head saying, "Mind your business."

As I slipped on something comfortable to wear and was sliding on my shoes, I heard Ian's voice in my head again, "Mind your business."

It was at that time that I became frustrated with that phrase replaying over and over, so I responded out loud to no one, "*Shut up*, Ian!"

Just as I said that, Ian walked into the room. He looked at me with a confused expression and unzipped his hooded sweatshirt.

"Why are you telling me to shut up?"

I almost leapt to the ceiling at the sound of his voice. I spun around with my hand over my heart to keep it calm.

"Oh, my God, Ian! I didn't even hear you come in." I reached for my purse.

"Yeah. Now why did you say 'shut up, Ian?'" he asked.

"It's silly. That's all."

"You going out?"

"Yeah," I sighed and slowed down to talk with him. "I got a message from Hailey. She said that Steve didn't come home last night."

Ian shook his head and tossed his sweatshirt on the floor next to the laundry basket. He peeled off his sweatpants and looked scrumptious in his boxer briefs and wife beater. His chest glistened with sweat as he pressed his lips together with frustration.

"Josephine, baby, I told you to mind your own business."

"I know. I've been hearing your crazy voice in my head all morning. That's why I said to shut up."

When he heard my explanation he smiled.

"Glad I have that effect on you." He moved his sweaty body close to mine. "So where are you going?"

"To see her."

"Alright, Josephine," he said as he lifted his arms in surrender. "I can only offer advice. Do what you want." He kissed me goodbye and rubbed my shoulder gently.

"Oh, and try and be back by seven okay, baby?" he asked.

"Okay."

Ian must've had something planned because he never requested me to be home at or by a certain time. I wondered what he was up to. Knowing Ian, he was probably preparing a new dish that he needed a guinea pig for. It seldom mattered to me because everything he made was delectable.

After I left sweaty Ian, I managed to reach Hailey on the phone. She refused to go into details over the phone and just instructed me to come over to her house. I turned the steering wheel slowly onto her street when I saw the signs indicating where her house was located. Although I had been over to her home several times, instinctively, I was driving cautiously. It was as if it was my first trip there and I was afraid I'd miss seeing her house number.

When I finally arrived in her driveway I parked my car, but I did not turn off the ignition right away. I wasn't quite sure what to expect when I walked into her house. I was trying to prepare myself for every possible scenario. Would she be in tears? What if he arrived? Was she angry and getting rid of his things? I had no idea. After a while, I shut off the ignition, strapped my purse on to my shoulder and let myself out of the car. I took a deep breath before knocking on her door. It took a while for her to answer, but I waited patiently because I knew she was there. When she answered the door, she looked like she had been crying.

"Hailey?"

"Come on in, Josephine."

I sat on her sofa and she sat in the chair across from me. She had an empty bottle of merlot on the coffee table and the wine glass next to it was partially full.

"You been drinking all morning?"

"Girl, damn near. His phone is off and he hasn't called me yet. You know, I hope he's alright, but my gut is telling me he was with someone. I can only get but so mad, right? It's karma. I've been seeing someone else behind his back. It was bound to happen, right?"

"Let's not jump to conclusions." It was the only thing that I could think of to say. Even still, I kept hearing Ian's voice, which I wanted to heed, but my girl was in pain. She had pretty much drunk a whole bottle of wine and it wasn't even eleven o'clock yet.

"I feel so out of control, Josephine. I gotta get out of here or I'm going to go crazy wondering what he's doing or if he's dead!"

"Did you leave him a message? Where do you want to go?"

"I called my friend, so I'm going over to his house."

I pressed my hands on my temples as I tried to understand the logic behind that decision and why she would wait to leave after I drove over there!

"Hailey, do you think that's a good idea?"

"Does it *really* matter?"

Hailey stood up and went to her hall closet to get her jacket. She stuffed a few tissues in her purse and made sure she had her keys in her pocket. I stood up and slowly walked to the door to let myself out because there was no need in trying to reason with her — she had her mind made up. For some reason, I just didn't see her and

Steve apart. It seems the longer you are in a relationship, more and more tests are thrown your way that measure your love and commitment to that person. For the fortunate ones who pass with flying colors, they realize they have someone who is true to themselves and someone who will be true to their mate. For the ones who fail, perhaps that person is not right for them no matter how hard one tries to hold on to them. Steve and Hailey had been together for so long that I just thought that they had already endured the worst. Apparently, I was wrong.

CHAPTER 13

By noon, Tamar's cell phone was ringing. The electrical device successfully interrupted the Saturday that she planned to take full advantage of. On Saturdays, pre-resignation, Tamar would get her hair and nails done and then run some much needed errands. Since today would mark the end of her third week of unemployment, post-resignation, she would have to settle for a day at the law library.

The peace and quiet of the law library was shattered when her cell phone rang. She tried to silence it quickly by answering it, but it was at the bottom of her purse. In the distance were a few scattered huffs and sounds of lips being smacked apart in disgust. Her immediate concern was to answer the phone, not to put anyone in check like she was often inclined to do.

"Hello?" she whispered into her device, covering her mouth to amplify the sound for the unknown caller.

"It's Donovan. How are you?"

"Oh, hey there. I'm good."

"What are you doing today?"

"I'm at the law library," she told him as she gathered her things and headed toward the exit.

"You want to go to Pentagon City Mall with me when you're done? I need to pick up this pair of shoes. Then we can grab a bite to eat in Shirlington."

Tamar opened the door to the exit and stood there for a moment as she looked out at the blue sky. She enjoyed the solitude, but it sucked when she didn't have any money to spend. Sure she had enough saved to last her a full twelve months without working, but that money was used just for the bare essentials — which meant no shopping sprees, no nail repairs and no visits to the spa. At least she could enjoy watching someone else spending their money.

"Uh, sure. Can you pick me up?" she asked. "I took the train out to GW University."

"Okay, baby. I'll be there in about twenty minutes."

Tamar felt like this may be a good opportunity to get whatever was bothering her about Donovan off of her chest. She knew if she did that she would feel better and it was only fair to him. She loved his company and always wanted to see him, but did not feel compelled to be committed to him. She struggled subconsciously over why she denied allowing herself to be closer to him by having a more steady relationship.

When he arrived at the university, she hopped in his car and strapped on her seatbelt. Donovan leaned over to get a kiss from her and she obliged. She looked straight ahead as Donovan drove. He turned down the volume on his XM Radio jazz station just before he spoke.

"You okay, baby?"

"Donovan, you know me. And you know I don't bullshit anybody and I'll speak my mind."

"Right, baby. What's up?"

"I don't know what's wrong here. I enjoy you, I enjoy the sex, but I feel smothered. What bothers me is when I'm away from you all I do is think about you."

Donovan kept his hand on the steering wheel and looked straight ahead. His eyelids dropped a bit and he turned his head to the left to check the side mirror. After he looked for nothing in particular, he then turned his vision back to the road.

"What is it?" she asked him.

"I think I have an idea." He rubbed the back of his neck with his free hand and sort of chuckled to himself.

Tamar became attentive to what may become some insightful wisdom regarding her issue with him. "I'm listening."

"Tamar, I really love the fact that you keep it real," he said as he made an illegal U-turn. "But I also love that I can be real right back at you and you not take offense. That's first, but, baby, I think you are still upset because of what happened at your job."

"*Your* job," Tamar corrected him with a bit of sarcasm. She hated the fact that he had pinpointed the problem so quickly.

"My job, your job, the job I have now, whatever. You resent that I'm in that job, that we are boning, that you haven't found a job yet, and you're not in control," he stated.

Tamar was silent as she waited for him to continue.

"No, you *really* hate the fact that we are boning and that you enjoy it. You're mad at yourself, baby, and you're taking it out on us. That's not right."

Tamar looked down in her lap. Donovan was right and she knew it. It was not just her feeling forced out of her job, it was the fact that she was sleeping with the man who she felt took her job away from her.

"Understand that I didn't know you and I didn't know your boss. I don't know why they didn't give you a partnership, baby. But it's not my fault. I really care about you, baby, and I want you to be happy. If I'm not adding to your happiness then we need to end it. I'll be honest with you, I don't want it to end. I want to see how far we can go with one another."

"You do make me happy, Donovan. And you're right, I am mad at myself and mad at the situation. I know it's hindering us. What do we do?"

"Why don't you call that lead I gave you so she can hook you up with a job? She can get you in, but you still have to prove yourself, so it's not like a total handout. Don't be proud, baby. I really want to be with you. From the moment I first saw your pretty, but angry face."

Tamar and Donovan laughed as they reminisced about the first time they met.

"Okay, Donovan, I will call this woman, get this job and not make you look bad. I want to apologize too. I know it's not your fault."

"And you *really* didn't have to quit, but that's another story."

"What do you mean? You ate me out on top of your desk and we got busy up against this huge window overlooking K St. I *had* to leave! And you kept my drawers!"

Donovan laughed about the day they first met as he caressed her leg gently. Tamar leaned over and kissed him on his cheek. She was relieved that she could be so candid with him without him resenting her for it. Now that they had overcome this towering hurdle in their relationship, she was sure that everything else with them would be just fine.

It was that day that Tamar respected and loved Donovan.

CHAPTER 14

Hailey tried not to cry on the way to her friend's house. She wanted to look fresh for him and give him the appearance that nothing was wrong. She had not felt so much confusion all at once before. She was disappointed with Steve while traveling to another man's house to find solace and be soothed.

Hailey pulled into his driveway and sat in her car for a moment. She knew in her heart that she needed to end things with him, but couldn't bring herself to do it. The pain of Steve not coming home, which was a first in a long time, was not as deep as it could've been because of her extra curricular activities with her male friend.

Hailey's friend must have heard her car when she pulled into the driveway because she noticed that his door was opening slightly. She checked her face in her visor mirror. Her eyes were a little puffy and slightly reddened. She made herself smile and instantly her face looked 100 times better.

"Okay, Hailey," she told herself. "You can do this."

Her friend unlocked the door so that Hailey could let herself inside his house. She slowly walked in and hung up her jacket in his coat closet. There was an old Motown song playing on his stereo by Smokey Robinson and the Miracles, "Ooh Baby Baby."

Hailey looked over her shoulder and noticed him sitting on the couch wearing red, silk boxers. She smiled at his attempt to be romantic and took a deep breath.

"Bryan Bryant," she told him. "You are always full of surprises."

CHAPTER 15

Since I was ousted from Hailey's presence, I decided to call Camilla. She was the last person seen with Steve. I was beginning to feel like a detective as I tried to locate Steve's whereabouts for my friend Hailey. Not to mention, I had been driving from town to town and still had a pounding headache. Camilla's phone rang four times before she answered.

"Camilla? Hey girl, what are you doing?"

"Excuse me. Since when do you call me asking me what I'm doing?" she chuckled. "What happened to *how* are you doing?"

"Sorry. How you doing? Now, *what* are you doing?"

"I'm just chilling out, cleaning up around the house."

I told Camilla that since I was already out and about that I would be stopping by her house in about fifteen minutes. Yes, it was bold of me, but I was doing this for the sake of my friendships with everyone involved.

I walked in her house and she was holding a huge feather duster. She had on tear-away gym pants with the buttons down the side of the leg and an oversized sweatshirt. Even though her hair was in a ponytail, she had several fly-aways around her hairline. She looked like a kid at the end of a rough day of kindergarten.

"*Well?*" I egged her on.

"Well what?"

"What happened?"

"What happened with what?"

"Don't play with me, Camilla. What happened with the guy you were with? Did you guys like . . . you know?"

"Josephine, you are just too damn nosey."

"Noted. Now just answer the question."

Camilla laughed and continued to do her dusting. She ignored me and she knew that there was nothing more that I despised than being ignored. She just held this silly smirk on her face and she knew that it irked me, so I played it cool, sat down and watched her dust for a while. I could tell from the way she deliberately switched her narrow ass around, trying to be funny, that she and Steve had gotten busy.

I watched her for about three more minutes and decided to betray Ian's instructions when I told her, "Be coy all you want, but I know that guy."

Immediately Camilla stopped dusting and looked over at me with her jaw slacked. I figured that little tidbit would snatch her back to reality.

"*What?*" she boomed. "Who is he?"

I looked at my nails and whistled some tune that I made up as I basked in the news that I had just given her. I wanted to enjoy the fact that she was probably packing her underwear with that news.

"Oh, no one," I sang out. "I'll just keep my nosey mouth shut."

"Touché. Josephine, if you know this guy, you gotta tell me!"

I got up from my seat and walked around looking at her belongings and various little trinkets. Every now and then I ran my finger across a surface and rubbed my fingertips together to indicate that she missed a few dusty spots.

"Oh, Josephine, that's messed up," she stood with her hands on her hips. The feather duster was sticking straight out at her side as if it were part of her anatomy.

"I know it's messed up, Millie. I think I'll just wait for this thing to unfold."

"Well, it was just one night. I wanted to get back at Bryan. Do you know I called him this morning and he didn't even answer his phone? What a joke. Even if I did get back at him, he probably doesn't even care."

With that revelation, she flopped down on the couch and began sulking. She rested her head in her hands for a moment before she spoke. I can only imagine that she probably felt used regardless of the fact that she tried to use someone too.

"All I did was screw somebody just to prove that I could, but it doesn't even matter. Now you know the dude? Who is he, Josephine?"

"He's a friend of mine. That's all."

"Is he a creep?"

I chuckled before I spoke. "No, girl, but he's in a relationship — a serious one at that. That's why I'm a little surprised that he would hook up with someone else. He told you that he was involved?"

She nodded with her head still in her hands. Then she lifted her head and looked up at me.

"But I didn't care! I wanted some beefcake and got it. End of story."

"So you're not gonna see him anymore?" I asked, hoping secretly that she wasn't going to.

"I don't plan on it. I think I'm gonna try to straighten things out with Bryan," she claimed.

"Why do you want to straighten things out with Bryan? I thought you were kinda pissed with him? You know, the whole Tupperware night thingy?"

"Yeah, but, I'm gonna give him another chance. Maybe I should go over there."

I pondered her comment for a moment before I fully realized what she was saying. Busy with trying to understand why she wanted to "work things out" with someone like Bryan, who clearly just wanted her for sex, not even good sex at that, boggled my mind.

"Wait. You're just gonna show up at his house? I thought you called and he wasn't there?"

"And? I'm going over," she affirmed. "He's there. I know he is."

"Don't do that," I told her. "You wouldn't want anyone doing that to you. You almost bit my head off earlier when I told you I was on my way. Let's go to the mall or something."

Camilla huffed and stood. When she was to her feet, she threw the feather duster to the floor and stomped toward her bedroom to get herself ready.

"You always have to be the rational one!" she yelled at me.

"You have some headache medicine?" I shouted toward the bedroom.

"Uh, there's a bottle of scotch in there, that's about it!"

Great, I thought to myself.

Camilla threw on a pair of jeans and a light sweater and was ready in about ten minutes. She had foregone the full makeup, which was a surprise. However, she gave her face a light dusting with some facial powder, which gave her a matte finish. To me, she did not need the makeup, but she enjoyed getting all dolled up, she once told me. It made her feel more confident for some reason. She decided to drive, which was a relief for me since I had been driving all morning long. I kept my eyes closed while she drove us around.

My headache subsided somewhat during the drive and I was totally thankful for that. Because it was one of those "stealth" headaches, I knew once I stood up to get out of the car, it would be back aggressively. As the radio played, I told Camilla a few additional details about Steve as I kept my eyes closed lightly. The conversation and the drive was going so well that I opened my eyes partially when it felt like we were slowing down arriving to our destination. I slowly sat up when I realized we were in a neighborhood.

"Uh, what are we doing?"

"Just a quick stop," she responded lightly.

"Camilla? I know you are not just gonna pop up over Bryan's house! This is crazy. He is not your man like that, girl. I'm staying in the car."

"Josephine, please chill? I just want my Tupperware, that's all. Alright?"

"They sell Tupperware everywhere. Even at that crusty dollar store around the corner from your house. Are you *that* attached to plastic?" I rationalized.

"Yes." She parked the car near his driveway. There was another car in his driveway, so apparently he had company.

"Come on," she ordered me.

"No way."

"Please, Josephine?" she whimpered.

I stared at her for a moment as if she had hair like Don King. I was unsure if she was trying to control Bryan or if she was just a glutton for punishment. It was clear this man was seeing someone else. Never mind the bad sex and Bryan never taking her anywhere, the proof was the other car in the driveway. What other confirmation did she need?

"Why are we here? And stop telling me it's for the Tupperware!"

Camilla took a deep breath and stared at Bryan's closed front door for a moment before she spoke. She swallowed hard to fight back the threat of tears.

"I just need to see for myself, okay?"

I sighed heavily and unlatched my seatbelt. I understood what she meant. For some people feeling the pain from the visual of seeing the person they care about with someone else was what they needed to move on with their lives. A long time ago before Ian, I, at one time, was one of those people.

"Damn, girl," I proceeded. "Let's go. I do not want any drama."

As we headed up his walkway I looked at the car parked in his driveway more closely. It looked familiar to me, but I dismissed the notion by shaking my head and pressing forward to the door of where Bryan Bryant resided.

Camilla rang the doorbell. After a few seconds, she rang it again, pressing the buzzer three times. She paused for a few more moments and then she balled up her fist and pounded on the door. Hard.

"Was that the official police knock?" Camilla asked me for verification.

I was too busy staring at the car in Bryan's driveway to answer her. I was preoccupied with trying to convince myself that it couldn't be Hailey's car. I never took the time to memorize her license plates and, hell, I'm sure the manufacturer had the crazy idea to make money by creating more than one black Acura. Surely, it was just a coincidence.

Camilla pounded even harder the second time.

"You know what? He is busy. Let's go."

"I just want what belongs to me. And if he's busy, what is he busy doing?" she meandered her neck to emphasize that she didn't care.

The door opened and Bryan was standing there in a red, silk robe that was loosely tied at his waist.

"Camilla, what are you doing here?" he raised his voice a little.

"I came to talk to you and to get my Tupperware."

"You brought Jacqueline with you?" he pointed to me and contorted his face to show his disapproval at Camilla's bad choice.

"Uh, it's *Josephine*," she defended me, but I didn't care about him calling me by the wrong name. I hadn't planned on seeing or speaking with him again after this incident.

Bryan continued to talk through the door. "Wait here. I'll get your Tupperware."

"No, let me in, Bryan."

"Hell no! You just wait here," he snapped. "I'll be right back with your little Tupperware."

"Who's your friend *this week*, huh?" she yelled through his storm door.

I placed a hand on Camilla's arm signaling to her that she needed to calm down. Bryan was sure to call the police if she didn't ease up and I refused to be arrested today over this foolishness.

Just then, Bryan's 'friend' came from the rear wearing the matching top to his silk robe set.

"What the hell?" Camilla said as she grabbed my arm and forcefully pulled me in front of her to get a look at his friend.

I almost lost my balance and tumbled to the ground due to her almost yanking my arm out of the socket.

"Damn, girl, you crazy?" I asked as I snatched my arm from her grasp. I looked into Bryan's house and almost passed out anyway from what I saw. Sure enough, there I was staring face to face with Hailey.

Hailey stood frozen as she was stunned to see Camilla and me. Camilla was just as shocked as she shook her head slowly in disbelief.

"What the hell is your girl doing here?" Camilla asked. She tried to open the storm door, but it was locked. She yanked on it forcefully in an attempt to open it to get inside.

I shrugged. "Hailey? What are you doing here?"

"No, what are *you two* doing here?" Hailey's voice was muffled by the storm door as she stood with her hands on her hips now.

"You know these girls?" Bryan turned to Hailey and waited for her answer. When Hailey didn't respond fast enough for Bryan, he got upset with her. "What the hell is going on? Get your stuff and leave. Please, just go!"

"What?" Hailey asked. "Why are you getting upset with me? I didn't tell them to come over. No one that *I know* even knows about you!"

"You rotten bastard!" Camilla yelled out as she kicked the door. I know her foot must've been throbbing after that blow. She may have broken a few toes behind that punt.

"Hey!" he shouted back. "You do that again and I'm calling the police on you. Now get outta here now. You're a lousy whore and a sad bitch! Just get off my porch!"

Camilla, completely destroyed by his comment, immediately had tears well in her eyes. Her lip quivered as she fought the urge to begin wailing right on his stoop. She bit down forcefully on her bottom lip. I could tell she did not want to give him the satisfaction as she began breathing heavily. I looked at Bryan in utter dismay wanting to shatter the glass for crushing Camilla's feelings just because he was busted.

A few tears rolled down Camilla's cheeks as she approached his storm door closer and stared dead in his eyes. She bit her bottom lip again and mouthed the words "fuck you" and then ran off of his porch and back toward her car.

I shook my finger in a scolding gesture as I shot a convicting look at Bryan. I waited for Hailey, who was out of Bryan's house in less than a minute. She zoomed by me and then flung her items in her car.

"Hailey, wait!" I called out to her.

She revved her engine and backed out of his driveway, leaving tire tracks on the concrete.

I jogged over to Camilla's car that she had already started. She latched on her seatbelt and dabbed her eyes with the back of her hands. When I reached the passenger side door, she sped off.

"Camilla!" I called after her. "Ian told me to be home by seven! Damn!"

CHAPTER 16

By the time Steve had gotten home it was around one in the afternoon. He grabbed himself a drink from the refrigerator and almost chugged all of the container's contents in one swill. He lifted the remote and turned the TV to ESPN to get the latest sporting highlights. Immediately, an excited male voice boomed through the speakers as he explained the most riveting and jolting plays of the games the night before. With his eyes still focused on the television, Steve slowly walked in the direction of his caller I.D..

"Oh! That was sweet!" Steve shouted once the replay was over.

He glanced down at the caller I.D. and noticed that Hailey called him at three in the morning and again at five.

"Damn," he said out loud.

He picked up the phone and called Hailey to see if she was at home, but there was no answer there. He paused for a moment to think of where she could be. He then tried her cell phone, but Hailey's voicemail came on before it even rang.

"She's pissed," he said to the phone as he held it by his side and looked at the color display. He decided to call his friend Ian to see what was on his agenda for the day, if anything.

"What's up?" Ian said when he heard Steve's voice.

"Are you and your girl doing shit today or can you hang out?"

"Man, she's out with Hailey or one of her other girlfriends. Probably getting in folks' business. What's up?"

"Oh, okay. I was gonna go shoot some hoops. You wanna roll? We'll grab a drink afterward."

"That'll work. I'll meet you at the court in 20."

Steve felt a little relieved that his friend's girlfriend could possibly be hanging out with his girl. However, his random indiscretion teamed with Hailey coincidentally not answering the phone didn't feel right to him. In some dark corner of his mind is where he swept aside the bad feelings he harbored until he could speak with Hailey face to face. Until then, he didn't offer too much thought to it, but still felt uneasy about cheating on her.

By the time Steve met up with Ian, Ian was warmed up and ready to hoop. He already had his morning run and craved more exercise.

"What up, man?" Steve asked as he slapped Ian's hand loudly and pulled him in with a quick shoulder-to-shoulder hug.

"I can't call it, man." Ian replied. "You ready?"

"Let's go."

The guys obtained a pickup game and played three on three against guys who were a bit younger than they were. Ian and Steve still gave the youngsters a run for their money, but most of Steve's shots were noticeably off. He shot a few air balls and had so many bricks the guys teased him that a construction company could use his help in building a few houses.

After they lost that game, Ian stared strangely at Steve as he watched him pull himself together from the embarrassing loss.

"Something wrong, man?" Ian asked him as he laid his towel around his neck.

"Nah. I'm cool. Just off today." Steve grabbed his towel and wiped his head and face roughly.

Unconvinced, Ian took a huge swig of his Gatorade, swished some around in his mouth and recapped his jug. "Sure? 'Cause usually you ball like Kobe, but today you were playing like my little niece."

"Forget you, man!" Steve huffed and took a long pause before he exhaled and said, "Man, I love Hailey."

Ian looked at him strangely. "Okay . . ."

"I *will* marry her as soon as I get a few more things together for us. I really do love her."

"You going somewhere with this?"

"I cheated on her for the first time in a very long time. And the thing about it is I don't know why. Hailey's been great — she doesn't pressure me, she's supportive — she's good to me."

"So why'd you do it? I mean, Camilla is fine and all, but you and Hailey have been together through the Dark Ages." Ian took another swig of his Gatorade and started in the direction of his car.

"I know. That's what bothers . . ." Steve flung his towel over his shoulder as he began to follow Ian. Steve stopped in his tracks and confusingly looked at Ian with a slight tilt of his head. "Hold up. How'd you know about Camilla?"

Ian turned to face Steve. "Did I say Camilla?" Ian tried to back peddle, but unfortunately, Steve was not second-guessing his hearing or Ian's diction.

"Hell yeah, you said Camilla! How you know her?"

"Ah, man, damn!" Ian exclaimed as an indication to Steve that he did not intentionally mean for this lips to get so loose. "That's one of Josephine's girls. We saw y'all at this jazz place yesterday. You didn't see us, though."

"What the hell, man! So Josephine knew what was up and didn't say nothing? What's up with your girl?"

"Wait, wait. Don't put this on Josephine. One, I told her to mind her business and two, what are you doing cheating on Hailey anyway?"

Steve forcefully stuffed his items in his gym bag. Ian waited for an answer, but Steve continued to complete the task at hand. He couldn't answer Ian because he did not have a legitimate answer for him.

"Shit! What if they start talking?" Steve finally blurted.

"Would you rather Hailey hear it from you or from Camilla by accident?"

Steve shook his head and headed off the court with Ian on his heels. After about ten paces or so, Steve suddenly ceased his gait and Ian ran into him almost toppling Steve to the ground. Steve turned and faced him.

"Wait," he realized, "you mean Hailey knows Camilla too?"

Ian scratched his head. "I think so."

"Awwww!" Steve whined.

"Well, Josephine had a get together and I think they both met each other there. I think she said that all of the girls got along really well that night."

"Well, look, I ain't saying nothing, man. I can't lose Hailey to no trick. It was a one-time thing. Plus the sex wasn't even that great."

"It's on you. I'm sure Josephine already knows, but I told her to stay out of it and I'm not going to say nothing. If Hailey finds out, she's not gonna hear it from us." Ian unlocked his car door and threw the almost empty bottle of Gatorade on the floor.

"Hailey called me late last night and I wasn't home. I tried her today and she's not answering. It's like she knows something."

"Calm your paranoid self down! You can do one of two things; you can panic and not say anything and let the ax fall where it will, or you can calm your cheating ass down and be straight up and tell her."

CHAPTER 17

Here I was stranded in a nice neighborhood without my cell phone and without my handbag that contained all of my survival goods for that matter. After I looked to the north, south, east and west in despair, I accepted the fact that I really had no other alternative at the moment. Sluggishly, I shamefully walked back to Bryan's house.

"I can't believe this," I mumbled to myself. "I'm the only one *not* cheating and I get stranded. That's just not right."

I pressed the doorbell and stood in front of Bryan's door as if I were his friend. I tried to plaster a smile on my face in case he was peering through the peephole at me. After about thirty seconds, the door opened and he looked at me with bewilderment.

"Jacqueline? What are you doing back here?"

I brushed off the fact that he called me Jacqueline again. I couldn't get upset because I needed this favor. So I smiled instead and interlocked my fingers while I spoke with him.

"Bryan, I know this is awkward, but they left me with no way to get home or no way of calling anyone."

He stared at me as if I were speaking a foreign language. This arrogant man wanted me to go through the motions of explaining my case and then commence to pleading with him. I'm sure he knew what I was getting at before I even finished. I don't know what Camilla or Hailey even saw in him.

"Okaaaaay . . ." he drug out the syllable and retied his robe more securely around his waist.

"Well, I was wondering if you could give me a lift to Camilla's house. That's where my car is."

"Camilla's house?"

"Yes, and then I have to hope that she's there because my handbag is in her car."

He thought about it long enough for me to take a huge gulp and begin to sweat a bit under my armpits. Why was he putting me through this agony? I was only asking for a ride, not his left kidney.

"I suppose so," he finally said. "Come on inside."

"Thank you!" I stepped inside and stood near the entrance as to not appear too intrusive.

"Have a seat," he instructed. "I'll just be a minute." And with those words, he walked upstairs.

I plopped on his couch and looked around at his furniture, artwork and awards. He was an accomplished man. Yes, there was no denying that at all. I guess I could understand that this facet of him may have been what drew Hailey and Camilla to him. There were several pictures of him sprawled about the living room — a sure sign to me that he is all about himself. His book collection only consisted of "How To's." A few titles that jumped out at me were, *How to Get Rich, How to Be Successful, How to Organize Your Thoughts,* and *How to Be an Articulate Speaker.* I mean, this dude had every self-help book imaginable. I giggled to myself when I thought, *He should've had How to Not Get Busted By Two Women.* What a mess this was and now I'm in the middle. Now I know why Ian was telling me to mind my business.

Realistically, Hailey couldn't be upset with me. She's the one who decided to have the affair with Bryan. Not to mention she kept it completely under wraps. I didn't even know she was dipping out on Steve until she wanted to share that information. Because of that, Camilla couldn't be upset with me either. Not to mention I told her not to come over and disturb Bryan in the first place. As far as I was concerned, I was free and clear in this instance. I'm actually the victim!

"Ready, Jacqueline?" he asked as he quickly grabbed his keys.

I gave a defeatist sigh, stood and flatly responded, "Sure."

While we were driving to Camilla's, I thought my head would hit the dashboard from falling asleep. I never met anyone that actually listened to classical music. Not that there is anything wrong with that, but Bryan just seemed to be the type of person who desired to be something other than himself. I was happy for the brother's success, but based on his humble beginnings that he mentioned in his bio, it seemed as though he was trying to leave a big part of himself behind — for good.

He turned the volume down on Chopin and decided to make small talk.

"So, Jackie, how long have you known Hailey?"

"Bryan, my name is Josephine."

"Oh, goodness! Why didn't you tell me? I do apologize. So . . . *Josephine*," he stressed my name as if he wanted to pronounce it correctly, "how do you know Hailey?"

"We used to work together a long time ago and have remained friends. How do you know her?"

"I met her at a charity fundraiser. She was the most beautiful woman in the room. She had no idea who I was and seemed to not be interested, but I knew better."

He smiled to himself as I looked outside of my window and rolled my eyes up toward the sky.

"I knew I wanted to be with her."

I looked at him very strangely. Hailey must not have told him about her 100-year relationship with Steve. Even if she had, I sensed from Bryan's attitude that he would not have given it a second thought just like Camilla. They both just wanted what they wanted without understanding that there were consequences.

"Oh. How interesting," was all I could say.

"She could've been Mrs. Bryant, but after today's fiasco, well, I just don't think that's possible."

"Well, not to be meddlesome, but she really didn't do anything if you think about it." I felt like I was betraying Steve when I said this.

"I thought about that later. Truthfully, it is really you and Camilla's fault."

I folded my arms and looked at him like he was crazy. I was about to address this, but we had arrived at Camilla's house. Thankfully, her car was there and I could get my purse and take my self home to my man.

"Oh, goodness! She's *here!*" he said with anguish in his voice.

"Well, you don't have to go in, but you should talk to her. She really likes you a lot, but she isn't sure why her feelings aren't being reciprocated. If you don't want to be with her at least give her some closure."

He seemed to be pondering what I said for a moment as I opened the car door to let myself out of the classical bus.

"Thanks for the lift." Before he could say you're welcomed, I closed the door. The bitter truth was that he still disrespected both of my friends. He was dating two women at once, he wasn't being a man and he wasn't acting like a man by having two women. He was acting like a spoiled, insecure, greedy little boy. What an agonizing ride.

I headed toward Camilla's house and heard Bryan open his car door. He poked his head up from the doorframe and called out to me.

"Jacqueline!"

This dude still didn't have my name right. I dropped my shoulders and slowly turned to face him.

"Tell her if she wants to talk, I'll be right here waiting for her to let me inside."

"Yeah, yeah," I mumbled as I turned away and walked up Camilla's sidewalk. I pressed the doorbell and she quickly answered.

"Josephine, I'm sorry! I was so upset. I tried to call you, but your purse was ringing in my car!"

"Never mind that, heifer. Give me my purse so I can get out of here."

"I'm sorry! Please don't be mad at me," she pleaded.

"That . . . guy is out here wanting to speak to you." I held my hand out for her to give me my purse.

"Bryan?"

I nodded yes.

"No! I won't!"

"Girl, for all you put me through today . . . you better! I had to practically beg for a ride and then had to ride in the car with him and listen to ohhhh, hmmm, errrr, *HIM!*"

She handed me my purse and took a moment to think about it. "What would you do?"

"I'm officially no longer in it. Your dilemma, your decision. Peace!" I lifted my two fingers giving her the peace sign and jumped off of her porch.

When Bryan saw me walking back to my car, he peered out and called out to me again.

"Well, Jackie? Is she coming?"

I looked at him, waved and then said, "Bye!" I hopped in my car and drove off.

*   *   *   *

Thankfully, I made it back to the house well before seven. I was done gallivanting for the day and I still had a nagging headache. The plan for me would be to take a pill and rest for a while. My inner thighs were extremely sore, so perhaps the pill would help subside that throbbing feeling there as well. I'm not sure what Ian had in mind for us this evening, but I hoped it wasn't sex. I just couldn't take anymore right now.

When I pulled up to the house, I noticed that Ian's car was there, but it was parked differently, so he must have gone back out after me. I walked inside and Ian was relaxing on the couch. Although he was napping, the TV volume was up entirely too loud and the show was talking about how some woman was on trial for murdering her boyfriend.

Why was he watching this? I thought to myself.

I reached for the remote and turned the TV off. As soon as the deafening sound from the TV abruptly came to an end, Ian stirred and then he woke up.

"Hey Jose," he muttered as he stretched.

Ian had so many nicknames for me that I never knew what he was going to call me at any given time. "Jose," pronounced as if he were going to say my full name, was, by far, his favorite. He once called me Fifi and I immediately objected to that. I was not a poodle!

"Ian, what were you watching?" I asked as I tossed the remote on the couch by his feet.

"I don't know. It was watching me."

"So what'd you do today?" I asked. "Did you eat, sweetie?"

"I'm good." He turned his head away from the TV and into the cushions on the couch.

He looked so good lying there in his wife beater and basketball shorts. His chest bulged as it tapered down to his flat stomach. I made a disapproving face when I noticed one of his hands was shoved down his shorts. I suppose that made him comfortable. He was obviously tired and I was going to leave him alone as I prepared myself for a nap, but I was curious as to why he wanted me back at seven.

"Ian, baby?"

"Hmmm?" he mumbled, still not moving now that he was in a more comfortable position.

"Why'd you want me home at seven?"

He sighed heavily before he spoke. I guess slightly I was annoying him. After all, he did wake up at six this morning for his run.

"We have eight o'clock reservations at Ruth's Chris," he murmured.

I smiled at his thoughtfulness. It wasn't a special occasion or an anniversary. My baby just wanted to do something special for us. I tiptoed out of the living room and climbed the stairs to go to our bedroom. I took an aspirin and looked in the closet for something special to wear. When I found the perfect dress, I set it aside for later and laid down for my nap.

CHAPTER 18

Tamar was frantically searching for the perfect suit to wear to this interview. She took Donovan's advice and called the lead he had given her. The woman seemed pleasant on the phone and was anxious to speak with Tamar. She was so anxious about the prospect of hiring someone that she wanted to meet with Tamar in the early part of the afternoon.

Tamar printed a copy of her impressive résumé and commenced to preparing herself for the executive interrogation. It had been four years since Tamar interviewed for a position, but she knew the rules of the game. She was articulate; she could make light banter to make the interviewer feel at ease, she was educated and knew her work as well as her worth. This job was in the bag and Tamar was going to walk into the interview with the confident demeanor that said the job was already hers. Donovan left to go to work and she had not had an opportunity to tell him the news. She left a message for him to call her, but his assistant said that he would be in meetings most of the day.

Tamar tore the piece of paper from its pad where she scribbled down directions to the interview site. The interview was near Tyson's Corner, but the worksite would be in DC. She was glad that the traffic would be moderate since she would be meeting with her in the middle of the day.

After Tamar had gotten dressed, she hopped in her car and sped off to meet with Celeste Bacon. *What a name.* Tamar thought to herself. She decided to save the jokes for her girlfriends and Donovan.

When Tamar arrived, the receptionist was very pleasant, which was always a good sign. If the person that works in the front is not friendly, 95% of the time, the organization is not friendly. She never imagined that she would be interviewing again — at least not for a while anyway. She was so sure her partnership at her previous job was in the bag, but as she came to realize, things can and do change.

"Would you like coffee or water while you wait for Bacon?" the receptionist asked Tamar.

"No, thank you. I'm fine." Tamar chuckled on the inside. She believed the receptionist asked her in that manner to see if Tamar would laugh or correct her.

Even the receptionist smirked slightly after she formulated the question.

Not long after Tamar took her seat, Ms. Bacon rounded the corner in a fast gait, heels pounding hard on the carpeted floor.

"Tamar?" she asked.

"Yes, Ms. Bacon?" Tamar asked as she stood to greet her.

"Celeste, please. Nice to meet you," she extended her hand for Tamar to shake. After they exchanged firm handshakes, Celeste asked Tamar to follow her to her office.

Celeste was an attractive woman with very dark skin and a short, tapered haircut. Her physique looked like she hadn't been to the gym in a while, but, despite that, she could still turn a man's head with what she had.

"Have a seat," she instructed Tamar.

Tamar took a seat and was prepared to obtain the job.

Celeste reached inside her desk drawer and pulled out a pen to jot down notes on the résumé Tamar e-mailed her earlier that day.

"Okay, we are in need of someone to head our entire regional legal advertising and business sector. We have several clients under our belt and need someone who is sharp that can help revise their current legal contracts and issues in regards to advertising, but to also oversee class action suits, proprietary actions, etcetera. It is definitely two ends of the spectrum — you may be head counsel on most of the business cases, but seldom utilized on the advertising side of the house. The reason we need someone quickly is because the person who was in this position was asked to resign."

"Really?"

"Yes. He was sharing the corporation's marketing campaigns and trade secrets with several national competitors and getting paid for sharing those secrets. His trial starts next month. We are not representing him. Conflict of interest. Most likely he will be disbarred. Obviously we are also looking for someone who is discreet and can be a loyal contributor to our firm. With all of that being said, I'm glad you contacted me. Donovan told me that you were sharp and that you were looking for something in the very near future."

"Yes. I'm looking for a firm that will appreciate my input, give me the freedom to work independently and will challenge me as well."

"This is that firm. And I take it that you are also looking for a firm that compensates you for your hard work and can make you partner too, right?"

"That never hurts," Tamar smiled.

"Your résumé is extremely impressive and I've already spoken with your last firm."

"Really?" Tamar squinted her eyes at the action because that was unorthodox. "Are you making an offer?"

"What would your salary requirements be?"

"When I left, I was at $91 an hour, billing rates I cannot disclose. Since this position requires someone to cover a regional area, I think $101 would be fair."

Celeste didn't balk at Tamar's salary requirement. "Actually we would start you at $120 an hour with a complete medical and dental package, along with 401K and stock options. Along with that comes free membership to the country club and you get a free round of golf one weekend per month. We have a timeshare as well, but that will be in the welcome package. You will get a company car and company credit card for gas and incidentals. Sound good?"

Tamar swallowed hard and tried to catch her breath. She could barely believe her ears. She worked almost as hard at the last firm and didn't even have a parking space.

"It sounds wonderful," Tamar coolly replied.

"Great! Give us a few weeks to get your office in order. After that, you will have two to three weeks to interview and hire two new staff members that will work directly with you, so select some sharp people. We will also send your signing bonus in the mail to you." Celeste stood to her feet and extended her hand. "It was a pleasure meeting you."

"Same here. Thanks for your time today."

"Not a problem. I'll have the receptionist mail a packet to you that has all the information that you will need. But if you stop by her desk, she will have an offer letter for you to sign today. That way we can get that $5,000 check to you today in time for the weekend so that you can do a little shopping. If you need to contact me between now and then, you have my number. Glad to have you aboard!"

"Thanks, Celeste. I won't let you down."

"I'm sure you won't. See you in a few weeks!"

Tamar left the office feeling confident on the one hand and a bit apprehensive on the other. She knew that she was a hard worker who was often referred to as a legal eagle, but *that* was just too easy. It was as if Tamar had driven to Tyson's Corner just to be looked upon. The salary, however, kept her from questioning how she got the job and if it would be a good fit for her. For $120 an hour, Tamar intended to make it a fit. Still, something didn't seem quite right.

CHAPTER 19

Last weekend was by far a crazy one, but I was glad that it closed with Ian surprising me with dinner at Ruth's Chris Steakhouse. That night I tried to return the favor by surprising him with dinner, but that was a total bust. I was not a good cook by any stretch of the imagination. I burned the bread, but my baby did not complain, but he didn't eat them either. My apologies for destroying dinner fell on deaf ears. Ian kept telling me there was no need to apologize, that he enjoyed the effort, but would be handling all of the cooking from that point forward. So instead of feeling bad about dinner, I decided to give him a full body massage. He hinted around to wanting one earlier that day, so I obliged.

I had jazz playing softly in the background and the body oil close at hand for Ian's massage. He claimed he lifted weights incorrectly at the gym yesterday, but I knew better. He just wanted a massage. And usually when he wanted a massage, it was because something was on his mind and he wanted to discuss it with me.

"Relax, baby," I told him as he slowly lay down on his stomach and I straddled the backs of his thighs.

"Ah, thank you, sweetie. I need this."

"Umm hmm, I know." I remained quiet as I kneaded his flesh. He let out a few moans to indicate that my massage techniques were still pleasing to him.

"Babe, you like living with me?"

I lowered my brows and then smiled slightly. He couldn't see me, but I nodded because I knew he needed to talk about something important. However, I had no idea where this conversation was going.

"Sure."

"Do I do anything that gets on your nerves?"

"We've already talked about it," I told him. "There's no need to rehash any of that. Where is this coming from anyway?"

"Hmm?" he asked. He sounded like a drunken man about to fall into a hard stupor.

"Where is this coming from? Why are you asking this out of the blue?"

"Just thinking about Steve and Hailey."

"Okay?"

He lifted his body and I rolled off of him so he could turn around to face me.

"They've been together for a long time and that's all they have become — the couple that's been dating forever."

"That's not true," I defended. "Well, granted, yes, they have been together for a while, but they are comfortable with each other. They've been through a lot."

"Right, and he cheated on her and she cheated on him."

"True," I agreed.

"So something's not right," he concluded.

"Okay."

"You comfortable with me?" he asked me.

"Why do you do this? We are Ian and Josephine, not Steve and Hailey."

"I know, babe, but if something wasn't right, you would tell me, wouldn't you?" he asked as he interlocked his fingers in mine.

"I've never had a problem doing that before," I giggled and caressed his bare chest with the fingertips of my other hand.

"Thanks for my massage. Now take your clothes off."

"Ian!" I playfully hit him in his arm.

"I'm just saying. You were looking sexy when I came in from work today, I started to tear your clothes off right then and take you in the hallway."

"Oh, yeah?" I asked with a bashful grin.

"Hell yeah," he responded as he looked at me with seduction oozing from his eyes.

"Don't you ever get enough?"

"Of you? No way. Come here."

He gently pulled me toward him and kissed my lips softly. He lifted me up on his hips in one swift motion. I straddled him as our chests pressed gently against each other. I could already feel his manhood rising and stiffening as his kisses became more passionate and frequent.

He flipped me over carefully onto my back and unfastened my pants and began to shimmy them past my hips and down my thighs. He took his rightful position between my legs and nibbled roughly on my neck and shoulders. My back arched as my crevice moistened in preparation for him to enter me. And he did, gently and passionately.

As he slowly stroked in and out of me allowing me to feel every inch of his hardness, he looked in my eyes intently as if he had more to say to me. I caressed his face and he began to suck slowly on my thumb and kissed the palm of my hand. He pressed his body down next to mine and I knew that he couldn't contain himself any longer. His thrust became more powerful and rapid. I held on to him as tight as I could to prepare myself for my own climax. I could feel my pelvic area rippling as he thrust himself deeper and harder into me.

"Oh, Josephine," he moaned.

"Don't stop, Ian," I quietly commanded. As he continued to thrust, my demands became louder. "Don't . . . stop! Ohhhhh!!!"

"I won't, baby. Come!" His hot breath caressed my ear as his soft words poured out of his mouth. When he said that, he jerked the lower half of my body into his midsection and that sent me into a whirlwind of orgasms.

"Oh, God! Ian!!" I yelled out. When I said that, he squeezed me tightly toward him, which caused several more orgasms to release from my insides. I could feel my eyes roll back in my head as I squeezed them tightly shut.

I couldn't count the follow up orgasms that occurred over the next forty or so minutes. All I remember is not being able to control them.

"Oh Josephine, baby!" he managed to spit out just before his body contracted as he came.

"Oh, my goodness . . ." I said with a sigh.

"Oh, baby," he said just before he swallowed to moisten his throat. He rested on top of me for a minute to catch his breath and slowly rolled over beside me. He pulled my body closely toward him, which caused me to have a mini orgasm.

After that, I couldn't move. We both fell off to sleep, but not before Ian murmured, "Marry me."

CHAPTER 20

While Hailey was on the Metro train on her way home from work, she couldn't help but wonder what had gone wrong with her relationship with Bryan. After the incident on Saturday, she hadn't talked to Josephine or Steve. Steve contacted her Sunday and again on Monday, but she refused to take his calls. She was still a bit perturbed as to why he was unable to answer his phone at three and five in the morning. Since Steve and Hailey had keys to each other's place, Hailey was sure he would be making his way over to her house due to the fact that he hadn't seen her since Friday morning. Then she would be forced to confront him and explain her recent behavior as well.

For now, Hailey didn't want to tell Steve anything about Bryan because he didn't know about the affair and she felt there was no need to tell him at that time. In her mind, Hailey was convinced that she and Bryan's rendezvous were over. Bryan kicking her out through no fault of her own was a clear enough sign of that.

When Hailey inserted her key in the lock, she took a huge breath and turned the knob slowly. The aroma of vanilla from several lit candles instantly filled her nostrils. She inhaled deeply and smiled. She heard jazz playing softly in the background and tossed her keys on the table that served as a stage for several pieces of mail that was scattered atop it.

As she walked further into the house, she saw the dozen roses in a crystal vase on the dining room table. Steve was stirring something in a saucepan and took a moment to do a taste test. He nodded to himself to indicate his approval and then tossed the spoon into the sink. The stainless steel utensil clanged around loudly before it settled. He hadn't heard Hailey come in the house. She watched him for a moment as she peered at him past the kitchen wall. She did not want him to know she was watching him in case he suddenly turned.

Hailey concentrated on her man as a hint of concern stirred her. She saw Steve place both of his hands on the counter and bend over at the waist as he dropped his head low. He held that stance for what seemed like several minutes. Instinctively, Hailey wanted to go and comfort him and perhaps ask him what was wrong — maybe even offer to help him reach a resolve to whatever was on his mind. However, those instincts faded several months ago.

After a moment, Steve lifted his body, took a deep breath and got back to stirring his dish. Although Hailey slowly crept into the kitchen, she made sure not to startle him as she observed everything.

"What's going on here?" she asked.

"Hi," Steve said as he turned toward her. "I didn't hear you come in." He walked toward her and gave her a quick peck on the lips. "How was your day?"

"Not too bad. You?"

"I took the day off and spent it cooking this dish. I hope you like it."

Hailey kicked off her shoes and left them at the entrance of the kitchen. She leaned her body against the wall and smiled at him before she spoke.

"What exactly are you making?" she said with a chuckle. It was odd for her to see him in the kitchen.

"Uh, chicken marsala, noodles and French cut green beans. I hope you dig it. Have a seat."

"What is all of this for?" she asked as she sat at the head of the table. Steve had already had a place setting there.

"I hadn't talked to you in a few days, so let's talk," he said without hesitation.

Instantly, Hailey wondered if Josephine told Ian, and Ian in turn told Steve about her affair with Bryan Bryant. Right away, her throat became dry and her palms began to sweat. She had been with Steve for so long that she couldn't imagine what life would be like without him. Being without him wasn't something that she was totally prepared for. Perhaps, she thought, this was a long awaited proposal since they had discussed it on several occasions prior to now.

Unfortunately, the possibility of a proposal posed a problem too because she begun to develop feelings for Bryan. She had not intended to, her objective was to just sleep with him until Steve was ready to settle down with her. But the last few times she and Bryan had been together, she looked at him as more than just a friend with benefits.

"Sure. Whatcha wanna talk about?" Hailey asked as she unfolded her napkin and placed it in her lap.

Steve took her plate and arranged the food he prepared on it. After he prepared his, he placed the food in front of her and sat down in the seat next to her.

"I want us to eat first," he suggested.

"Let's talk while we eat, eh? You know I like to know what's going on," she reminded him.

"Taste it. Let me know how it is."

She obliged and released a soft expression of satisfaction by saying, "Mmm."

"You like it?"

"It's very good. You did a good job! Soooo . . . what's up, Steve?" Hailey said as she put her fork down and folded her arms across her body.

"You serious, baby?" Steve asked her and received a nod in response. "Please, let's just eat."

She exhaled heavily and began eating again. They ate for a moment in silence, with John Coltrane softly serenading the couple behind the noise of clanking utensils against porcelain. Hailey decided to start a discussion since he refused to indulge her curiosity. Something had been bothering her this weekend and she wanted to irritate him just as much as she was frustrated at that moment.

"So what was up with you this weekend?" she started.

"Me? You mean, me or us?"

"I said it right. You. What was up with you?"

"Well," Steve said with a tad of apprehension, "I was wondering what was going on with you, so I stayed out of your way."

"Would you like to talk now?" she harassed.

He pushed his plate away because he knew they both probably wouldn't have much of an appetite after the talk.

"Hailey, I love you. I want to be with you. I'm getting myself together so we can get married, baby."

He paused and she uncrossed her arms. Unimpressed with this sentiment, she tilted her head slightly because she heard this spiel at least twice before.

"Riiiight," Hailey offered just to keep the story moving.

"Baby, I messed up—"

Before he could finish, Hailey took a deep breath and tossed her napkin into the plate.

"Again?" she finished his sentence. She rolled her tongue around her mouth to loosen up the food particles that collected between her teeth. She scoffed and nodded her head.

Steve looked in her eyes and reached for her hand, which she allowed him to take. His eyes began to well up as he fought back his tears.

"Baby—"

"So that's what all of this is about? I fuck up so let me butter her up first before I drop the bomb on her?"

"No, sweetheart. Not at all."

"Steve," now she was fighting back her own tears, "what are we doing? What the hell are we doing here? Playing?"

"Hailey, I love you. I do, babe." He caressed her hand, but she yanked it away this time.

"No, Steve. We haven't loved each other for quite some time. Since the *first* time this happened. You want to be in a relationship, but you don't want to take total responsibility. Just end things here. Wouldn't it be easier for us to do that instead of heaping a ton of bandages on the same old wounds?"

"No. I'm not letting you go that damn easily. I messed up, it was a one time thing, that's that. I'd rather you hear it from me than—" He cut his words off.

"Than whom?"

Steve bowed his head for a moment and then looked up at her. He knelt beside her and placed his hands on her knees.

"Than who, Steve?" She pushed his hands off of her and scooted her chair back to stand up. She began pacing the floor and stopped when she looked back at him. "Hell, you done slept with someone that we know? Or that I know? Damn, you batting a thousand tonight. No wonder you wanted me to eat first! Who was it?"

"That's not important. What's important is that it won't happen again."

Hailey reached for her dish that still had food on it, but she didn't care. She slammed the dish on the floor as hard as she could to get her point across to him. The plate shattered into what seemed to be a thousand pieces. The marsala sauce splattered across the floor and on the base of the refrigerator and lower cabinets.

"Who is it, Steve? I'm *not* gonna keep asking you."

A startled Steve knew that Hailey and Josephine had been through worse conflicts and he knew that they would be able to work things out no matter how big or small. Steve decided to do the unthinkable — he did the first thing that entered his twisted mind — he lied. Steve felt that this lie would take a load of heat off of his ass that Hailey would be unloading on him. Sure she would still be upset with him, but not as much if he told her it was just another random chick that he used for one night.

That would be the final straw to screw up his and Hailey's relationship for good this time. *A lie like this may work*, he thought. It could backfire, but he decided to let it ride out until he needed to come clean with the truth. He decided to turn the focus off of him so he could work on fixing his relationship with Hailey.

"Steve!" Hailey raised her voice this time. "Who was it?"

"Oh, Hailey," he paused for effect, "it was Josephine."

"What?"

CHAPTER 21

After Tamar hung out at Tyson's Corner mall and picked up two new suits for her new job, she was on her way home. By now, she would be in the thick of rush hour traffic and she and Donovan would probably arrive at home at the same time. She wanted to have dinner ready for him to celebrate, but now she would have to throw something together quickly or just thank him for the lead to the job in other ways.

By the time she peeled off of traffic and onto the exit for her house, Donovan was already at home.

"Hey, baby," she greeted him with a hug and kiss.

"Hey, you," he said as he gave her a seductive look from head to toe. "Damn, you look good in that suit."

"Thanks, baby. How was your day?"

"Busy. I had a ton of meetings today. I got your messages, but couldn't call you back. After my last meeting, I left for the day. You wanna go out and get something to eat?"

"Yeah, that's cool. I got caught up in traffic. I wanted to have dinner ready for you to say thanks for referring me to Celeste. I got the job."

"You got it?" He hugged her. "That's good, babe. I'm happy for you."

"Yeah, but . . ."

Donovan loosened his tie and unfastened the buttons on his cuffs as he tried to understand what Tamar was about to say. "But what?" he asked her.

"But she didn't interview me. It's like she just called me in to look at me. She offered me the job right on the spot."

"Well . . . baby, I told her a lot about your qualifications. She saw your résumé and probably jumped on hiring you before some other company snatched you up." He put his arms around her for reassurance.

"I mean, I'm happy, but something didn't seem quite right about that."

"Babe, it's called a hookup." He laughed, gave her a squeeze and then released her from his grasp. "Let me hop in the shower and throw on something else. Then let's go get something to eat."

Tamar smiled, nodded and blew him a kiss. He smiled his hypnotic smile that melted her every time and then turned to get himself together.

When they arrived at the restaurant, the wait wasn't as long as it usually was despite the large dinner party toward the rear of the venue. It seemed to be a rowdy bunch, but it didn't bother Tamar in the least. She just wanted to enjoy her man and the fact that she had a new job along with a $5,000 check to come. From time to time she still struggled to push aside the fact that Donovan now had what should've been her job, but she knew now that it wasn't his fault. However, she still didn't feel quite comfortable with the "hookup," as Donovan called it, and tried her best not to think negatively about how she came to get the job.

"I haven't been here in a while, babe," Donovan said as he looked around to see if he noticed any renovations. "You've been pretty quiet. You okay?"

"Hmm, yeah," Tamar lied. "Just wondering what to expect on this new gig, that's all. So your meetings today, were they with any of my old clients?" She grinned and nudged him playfully.

He smiled at her and threw his arm around her shoulder to pull her in close. "As a matter of fact, yes. Some of them were. You remember Logan O'Donnell?"

"The sweat machine?"

Donovan laughed. "Yeah, that's him. What is his angle?"

"You mean, why he sweats so much?"

Donovan bowed his head and laughed then he gave her a kiss on her forehead. "No, sweetie. Why is he so apprehensive about every legal solution that we throw at him?"

"That's easy," she answered while caressing his back. "He thinks because he saw *A Few Good Men* that he's a lawyer, but he doesn't know squat. Next time, and every other time, just ask him how he would handle xyz at the next publicized meeting. He'll clam up in front of you, in front of everyone. After he sweats a few liters, present some sound legal advice that the rest of the staff is sure to agree with, then he'll listen and agree with everything you say from there on out. If he does it again after that, repeat the said objectives."

"He *does* kinda look like a low budget Jack Nicholson. Okay," Donovan smiled. "I'll try that next time."

Tamar and Donovan's table was close to the rowdy group in the rear. They were behind closed curtains, but their bad jokes and stories about their families could still be heard clearly.

The waiter came from behind the curtain with their bill and a huge smile on his face. Tamar didn't know if it was because he was happy that they would be leaving soon or ecstatic with the tip he would soon receive.

"Babe, we need to take a trip this year," Donovan suggested.

"Oh, that sounds cool. Hopefully the new gig won't be too demanding and I'll be able to travel."

He reached over and caressed her hand. "Where would you like to go?"

"Hmm, don't know yet."

"Spain? Would you like that?"

"Are you serious? Of course I would!"

Just then, the large party behind the curtain began to disperse and the noise level increased. Naturally, Tamar and Donovan were inclined to see who contributed to the sudden disturbance of the peace. Amongst the bunch was Celeste. She noticed Donovan first and then greeted Tamar.

"Donnie?" she beamed. "How are you, sweetie?" She leaned over and gave him a hug and kissed his cheek.

Donovan did not stand to greet her, but instead pointed in Tamar's direction. "You remember Tamar, right?" he said as he smiled at Tamar.

"Oh, yes. She is going to be our new legal eagle! How are you, dear?"

"Doing great," Tamar said.

"She is one sharp woman, Donnie, I'm glad we were able to snatch her up. So you guys having a business dinner?" Celeste inquired with a smile.

Tamar grinned slightly and decided to let Donovan answer that question.

"Uh, no, Celeste. This is my lady." Donovan took Tamar's hand and pressed his lips softly against it. He then smiled at Tamar and winked.

Tamar returned a smile and then looked up at Celeste. Celeste's disposition shifted slightly, but she recovered quickly as she looked at them.

"Oh, no, I didn't know that. My goodness." She placed one hand on her hip and the other on her chest as if to stop her heart from beating. "You didn't mention that today, Tamar!"

Tamar wore an obvious look of bewilderment at her comment. "Why would I?"

"I didn't mean it that way. I just . . . I had no idea," Celeste said with a smile. "Well, I'd better scoot. We'll see you in a few weeks, Tamar!" She extended her hand for Tamar to shake.

"Great! I can hardly wait," Tamar told her as she shook her hand.

Donovan said his goodbyes to Celeste as well by shaking her hand. "Celeste, it was nice seeing you again and thanks for taking care of Tamar."

"Not a problem at all. I'll talk to you soon, okay?" She leaned in for a hug while she still held on to his hand. She secured her purse onto her shoulder and looked back at Tamar with a smile. "You two enjoy your dinner."

Tamar's eyes followed her out as she left. She shifted in her seat a bit and sipped her water before she spoke.

"They also gave me a signing bonus," she said.

"Oh, that's what's up," Donovan signified. "Was it a good one?"

"Was it?" Tamar confirmed. "So you never told me how you two know each other."

"I didn't?"

"No."

"We used to go to law school together. We vowed to always have each other's back afterward no matter what."

Tamar nodded. She wasn't the sort of person to pry, but she needed more information than the two of them just going to law school together.

"How'd that come about?"

"What?"

"Having each other's back no matter what." Tamar sipped her water again. "What made you guys make that pact?"

"She helped me study for the LSAT, which I passed and I helped her get into law school by putting in a good word for her with the Dean. We went to undergrad together too."

"Oh, cool," Tamar offered. "Well, I'm sure she will be telling me all of your dirty little secrets once I start working there."

Donovan chuckled and buttered a piece of bread. "I wouldn't count on it."

CHAPTER 22

Camilla was overwhelmingly gratified again. She bought a huge bouquet of flowers for her house, a few new bra and panty sets, some pumps and, most importantly, a new set of Tupperware. She and Bryan Bryant decided to patch up their relationship the day she left Josephine stranded at his house. After Josephine zipped away in her car, Bryan stood on Camilla's doorstep pleading for her to let him inside so they could talk. Bryan knew that all he required was a private moment with Camilla and he would be forgiven. She tried to play hard to get, but he suspected that she would be unable to resist his charms but for so long. He was aware of what she liked about him and he intended to use those assets to his advantage. That day, Bryan and Camilla had a rather lengthy talk about what happened.

"How could you?!" Camilla asked once she let Bryan inside her house.

He stood on the porch for all of three minutes before she caved. At that moment, Bryan knew the rest would be a piece of cake.

"I didn't mean for you to find out that way," he explained.

"Oh, no?! You mean, you didn't *mean* for me to find out, period!" she argued at him with a single finger pointed straight in the air.

Bryan took both of Camilla's hands and escorted her to the couch so they both could sit down to speak civilly to one another.

"Camilla, please," he told her, "I care about you. Hailey means nothing to me. I want you."

Camilla silenced her rage for a moment as she absorbed the smooth batter of words that Bryan just poured over her ears.

"You do?" she asked with a doe-eyed expression.

"Of course I do," he admitted.

Camilla, now convinced that she was his number one, felt the need to come clean about her behavior that same weekend. She explained to him that his insensitivity had forced her into the arms of another man. Bryan seemed a bit astonished that she had set her feelings for him aside just long enough to screw someone else. Even though he knew he should restrain his emotions in that instance, he couldn't help but feel a bit cheated. His slightly bruised ego paled in comparison to his oversized arrogance. Still, the image of her being with another man bothered him and he was disturbed that he felt that way. To him, Camilla was just something to do.

Although Camilla was happy for the moment, she was still troubled by the fact that Josephine's friend Hailey had been delivering the goods to Bryan. She essentially blamed Hailey for Bryan's fear of commitment. She needed an explanation, which was the only way she could feel completely better about her budding relationship with Bryan.

"So," she pleaded, "can we start over again? I'm so sorry!"

"Certainly, my darling," he answered. "But you must never be with another man as long as we are together. I won't accept it again. I can't."

"I won't, Bryan! I promise!"

He patted her thigh as a gesture that he accepted her assurance. As he felt triumphant with Camilla's quick will to forgive him, he couldn't help but think of how Hailey would've handled the situation. He knew deep in his heart that Hailey would have never accepted that explanation. He began to strategize how to win Hailey back so she could be a part of his life again. She was the one he felt the most in tune with and emotionally connected to. He decided to give Hailey a little while to cool down before he tried to contact her.

"I just need to know one thing," Camilla started. "You know, since I know that you care about me and don't want Hailey . . ."

Bryan slowly acquiesced to Camilla's upcoming query by giving her a nod of his head.

"How long were you guys seeing each other?" she asked him.

"Camilla, I don't want to get into this with you, darling. Concentrate on us."

"I would like to, but it still bothers me, Bryan. For us to put it past us, we need to discuss it."

"I have to get ready for my book tour next week."

"What does that have to do with *this* conversation . . . right now?" she asked.

He took a moment to think of something to say, but before he could respond, Camilla continued.

"Just tell me how long?"

"Camilla, please. If I tell you how long then you're going to want to know if I enjoyed it. Then you'll want to know do I still think about her, will I get back with her, if we still talk . . . the questions will never end. I'm not in the mood for an interrogation."

Camilla folded her arms and stared at him briefly. She had no choice but to relinquish control in this situation. She couldn't demand him to tell her anything about what he and Hailey shared and she definitely couldn't make him tell her the truth. She nodded and flopped down on the couch beside him and, for once in their relationship, she gave in.

"You're right. You're absolutely right. The questioning would never end. I guess now I understand why you didn't seem too concerned with Steve. I got it." She crossed her legs and flipped through a magazine that was on the cushion beside her. She pretended to let it go, but Bryan wasn't buying that routine for a second.

"Now you aren't just telling me that for now and then you'll act differently, are you?"

"Of course not."

"Great! Are you still making dinner tonight? I'm getting hungry."

Camilla definitely was familiar with the one thing Bryan enjoyed from her and that was her cooking. When he asked her to make dinner, she took a deep breath and felt her teeth sink deeply into her tongue to refrain from saying something detrimental to their evening. Instead, she plastered on the best smile that she could manage given the current events that surrounded their relationship.

"I can make you a sandwich. That's all I've got in the fridge; bologna and cheese."

"Oh, Camilla . . . you have to work on that, darling. Shall we go out this evening?"

"Um, we shall." Camilla instantly became excited. "I'll be right back!"

She left to go put on a dress and sweep her hair back into a bun. Finishing off the evening by going to a fancy restaurant to celebrate being reunited on a new foundation was perfect in her mind. Deep down, she was also planning her method of attack as well. She thought this would be a great way to get a bit of payback even though she said she wouldn't. She told herself, *I will order the most expensive thing on the menu, two drinks, dessert and an appetizer! And NOT eat it all.*

When Camilla emerged from her bedroom, dressed flawlessly, not a hair out of place and wearing four-inch stilettos, there was little doubt that Bryan would not be impressed with how astonishing she looked. She could get into any exclusive members club the way that she was dressed. Not only that, she knew she would not bring a twinge of uncertainty to anyone's mind about who she was as she stood next to Bryan. She looked good enough to be shown off to his friends and colleagues in case they so happened to bump into any of them tonight.

Bryan looked at Camilla from head to toe before he commented. "Wow, you look great!"

"Thank you!" she told him as she extended her hand for him to take.

"You didn't have to get all dressed up for me," he admitted as he imagined what color underwear she wore underneath. He remembered now why he was initially attracted to her when she first approached him four months ago. She had a certain naughty sex appeal that intrigued him.

Bryan and Camilla hopped in the car and to Camilla's surprise they didn't travel far. Bryan slowed his car as he made his turn into the parking lot. He pressed the button to roll down the driver's side window.

There was static coming from the menu and it sounded like five or six people having a conversation about music videos before one of the voices asked, "May I take your order?"

Camilla lost her appetite.

CHAPTER 23

For the past few days, Hailey walked around in a daze. She still functioned normally, but a huge part of her was hidden from the world. Emotionally, she was numb by what Steve told her, while trying to logically justify how her friend could do such a thing. The day after Steve told her about what happened, Hailey knew she had to confront Josephine sooner or later, but was at a loss for words.

After all, Hailey had cheated too, so to what extent was her anger allowed? As she drove home from work passing several streets and cars that she was oblivious too, she decided to make a quick stop at the grocery store to load up on junk food. She planned to "veg" out on her couch and do nothing for the rest of the evening. Steve had been sleeping at his place since Monday because Hailey didn't want him with her at her place. But, again, if she wanted him to leave, it would only be fair for her to tell him of her affair with Bryan. Hailey also had to put her feelings for Bryan away for the moment. In addition to finding out that her best friend slept with her long-term boyfriend, Bryan had not contacted her since Saturday.

Hailey's emotions tossed and pivoted in and out of her head. This was her best friend they were talking about! How could she ask Josephine about Steve without getting completely upset with her, and how could she talk to her without having the affair with Bryan thrown back in her face?

She walked into the store and headed straight for the potato chip aisle. She perused the rows of Trans fat-free snacks and felt ten pounds heavier just looking at the colorful bags of crunchy treats.

"Hailey?" someone beckoned from over Hailey's right shoulder.

Hailey thought it was just her imagination, so naturally she ignored the male voice. She reached for a bag of chips that she never noticed before and began reading the nutrition facts on the back of the package. It mattered not to her at the moment, but it was a force of habit since she read about everything that she was consuming.

"Hey, Hailey? How you doing?" the voice asked.

Hailey turned around knowing now that her imagination wouldn't dare ask how she was doing. She noticed Ian and tried to smile, but her face couldn't muster the task. She tried not to take out her frustration with what occurred between Steve and Josephine on Ian. However, when she saw Ian, she felt undeniably nauseous. She wanted to dislike him because, at that moment, she saw Josephine in him. Consequently, Hailey's depression overrode her disgust.

"Ian," she said with a slow sigh. "Hey." She turned her back to him and resumed perusing the mountain of snacks.

"Hey, wait a minute. What's wrong? That's hardly the greeting you normally give me. What's going on?" Ian slid his cart out of the way of other shoppers before he placed his hand on her shoulder. He gently turned her toward him.

"If you must know, Steve cheated on me again."

Ian tried to act surprised because he already knew the story. "What? Oh, no."

"As if you didn't know," she said and rolled her eyes at him and turned away.

Confused by Hailey's response, he frowned, rubbed his eyes with his fingertips and shook his head. "Well . . . okay, yeah. I did know." He looked down, ashamed for lying so poorly before.

"How do *you* feel about it?" She turned to get Ian's response.

"Well, I mean, I don't know. There's really nothing I can do about it. That's between you and Steve."

"No, Ian!" Hailey raised her voice a little. "You and Josephine are in this too whether you want to be in it or not!"

"Whoa, whoa, whoa, hold it!" Ian lifted his hands from the cart. "I didn't ask to be in this. Josephine told me about it and Steve confirmed it. I think it's pretty sick. In fact, I'm the one that told him he needed to come clean with you."

Hailey stood confused as she tossed the bag of chips back on to the rack of goodies. As she folded her arms in front of her and studied Ian's face, the bag fell to the floor where it would remain.

"Josephine told you what happened?"

"Yeah, and I told her to stay out of it," Ian announced before he blew a raspberry. "For real, you and Steve have to work that out, not her." He leaned over the cart and propped his foot on its lower rail.

"Weren't you upset with her?"

Ian took a moment to think about it as he let out a soft groan and scratched his head. "Not really. I mean, I expected it from her. I think she likes to think she's helping, but not in this case."

Hailey huffed loudly and kicked Ian's cart with the heel of her foot. "Helping? Oh, she thought we needed help?"

Ian, startled a bit by Hailey's act of aggression, stood up straight and leaned against the shelves of snacks. "Well, it's hard to say. Steve was the one that Josephine saw, so—"

"What the hell kind of relationship do you two have?"

Ian gazed at Hailey with a confused expression when he took a few steps away from his cart. He wanted to be ready this time in case she decided to kick it again. She walked around Ian's cart stealthily as she approached him, her face just inches from his. Ian retracted his face away from hers; the sound of crunching potato chips ensued just above the nape of his neck. That was the only retreat available since his back was against a row of Doritos. He brought his hands up slightly in preparation to thwart off a slap in case she decided to take her anger out with Steve on him.

"I love her. After I leave here, I'm gonna drop this stuff off at the house and we're gonna go look at rings. She didn't tell you?"

"I haven't been taking her calls. And I'm surprised that you would marry her after she admitted to sleeping with your best friend!"

"What?"

"Yes, Steve and Josephine had sex! He said it was a one-time thing. What the hell? Why would she do that? How could he?" Hailey shut her eyes tight to keep her tears at bay.

"Nah," Ian shook his head emphatically. "Nah, nah, nah . . . I'm sure you got it all mixed up."

"I know what Steve said. He told me that he had sex with Josephine!"

"No, Hailey. I mean, why would he say that? Especially when it's not true!"

"Are you sure? Are you 100% sure?"

*   *   *   *

Ian drove home in silence. He trusted his woman, but Hailey threw a major curve ball his way. He didn't understand why Steve would tell Hailey that he slept with his woman. Ian knew that Steve had been with Camilla, but the more Ian thought about it, it seemed odd that all four of them were in the same jazz club that night. There was so much to do in DC and several different places to go. Truly, what were the odds of seeing someone whom you know so well on a random night? In fact, Josephine was the one that noticed the two of them that night in the dark and crowded lounge.

Maybe, Ian thought as he continued to journey home, *Camilla was being used to disguise Steve and Josephine's rendezvous in front of him. It was Josephine's idea to go there and they did not ride there together. What if Josephine and Steve met earlier that day and decided to part ways at the jazz club? Camilla could have been used as a distraction.* Ian shook his head at the notion and scoffed aloud at his absurd thoughts.

However, what if he was right?

When Ian drove into the parking space in front of his house, he sat there for a moment and stared at the front door wondering just who the woman was beyond it. It all seemed extremely illogical, but Hailey seemed pretty broken up about the situation. Not to mention she seemed decidedly convinced. Ian gathered the bags and headed inside. He didn't beat around the bush when it came to matters of the heart because he was too sensitive for that.

"Hey, baby!" Josephine greeted Ian with a kiss. "Oooh! You brought food! I love you!"

"Did you sleep with Steve?"

She backed away from him, tilted her head slightly and smiled. "What? What in the world would make you ask me that?"

"Did you sleep with him or not?"

"Of course not, Ian. Come on! Why would you even think that?" She grabbed the bags from him and headed toward the kitchen.

Ian slowly followed her, but he didn't know what to think now. Maybe she was being too calm as to not arouse any suspicion? Or maybe she felt embarrassed because Ian had just busted her out?

"Josephine, please—"

"Please what?" She turned from the counter and faced Ian with a serene look on her face as if Ian had never asked her about sleeping with Steve. It was ridiculous to her.

Ian gripped her shoulders tightly and pleaded with her to tell him the truth. "Josephine, baby, did you sleep with Steve? Look at me and tell me!"

She cupped Ian's face with both of her hands and kissed him softly on the lips. "Baby, please. Remember we saw Steve with Camilla. And who would tell you such a lie? It's not true. Whoever told you that is playing a sick, twisted joke on you and I'm not about to let them ruin our relationship over some mess!"

"I saw Hailey in the store. She told me that Steve admitted that he cheated on her."

"Well, good!"

"But she believes that Steve cheated with you. Steve told her he was with you, not Camilla."

"What?! Is that why I haven't been able to get in touch with her? That scared son of a . . . Why would he say that?" She walked over and grabbed the phone from the receiver. "We gonna end this right now."

Ian watched as Josephine waited for someone to answer the phone at their house. He looked like his whole world just came crashing down around him. She shook her head as their answering service blared in her ear.

"Hailey, this is Josephine. You need to call me. NOW! Ian told me about your conversation with him at the store. It's not true! And, Steve, if you get this message before her, you'd better tell her that you slept with Camilla or I will. Oops! I just did! What the hell is wrong with you, Steve?"

She slammed the phone back into the receiver.

Ian approached to give her a hug. He kissed her on the neck and squeezed her.

"I'm sorry, baby. It seemed strange, but Hailey was really upset in the store. She barely would talk to me!"

"You know what? Let's go over there. Is he crazy? How dare he lie to my friend, and then lie on me at that!"

"No, baby. Now you left a message. Just let it go for now. I'm sorry. I should've known better when she said that. I'm sorry. I didn't mean to grab your arm like that. You forgive me?"

I took a deep breath and touched Ian's chest. "Of course I do, sweetie."

"Good. 'Cause I'm gonna kill Steve."

"Ian!"

I walked away from him and headed toward the living room. I could feel a headache coming on as I flopped down on the couch and stretched my body out atop it. Ian was close on my heels. After I got myself comfortable on the couch for a catnap, Ian knelt in front of me.

"What's the matter, Josephine?"

"I'm trying to calm myself down before I get too upset over this. I like Steve and all, but it's one thing to suck at his relationship — now he has to try to ruin ours? You know what, let me just lie here for a moment and count to about 3,000 before my pressure goes up over this shit."

Ian leaned in to kiss my lips gently. "Umm, I'm not hungry, but if you want something, I can—"

"No," I interrupted him. "I just lost my damn appetite."

I inhaled deeply and held my breath for a few seconds before I exhaled. As I lay on the couch with my eyes closed, I tried to imagine that I was on a deserted white sand beach with crystal clear waters. As the surf broke the shoreline, teasing the specs of sand that would never touch the water's magnificence, I step to the cool water and allow it to cover my toes. The water retreats and I remain in the same place, wondering if the water would indulge me up to my ankles the next time it visited. It did. *Ahh!* I thought to myself. *I wish I were there right now.*

As I was about to immerse into a light sleep, the phone rang. I tried to ignore the one-sided conversation that Ian was having.

"Hello?" Ian answered.

I could hear him clearly from the living room as I forced myself to keep my eyes shielded.

"Yeah, she's here. Where is he? Well, did you talk to him? You two got my soon-to-be wife all stressed out for nothing! Get it straight. No! Get it straight. Hold on."

Ian walked back into the living room with the phone in his hand. I raised my forearm from my eyes and lifted my head a little to acknowledge his presence.

"Babe, it's Hailey."

I sighed just as I flopped my arm across my belly. So much for that catnap that I craved. I took another deep breath as I privately told myself not to be upset with Hailey. I'm sure she was a wreck after hearing from Steve that he cheated on her with her best friend even though it was untrue.

"Hailey? What has Steve told you? Oh, okay. . . yeah . . . yeah . . . I'll be here. Okay. Bye."

"She coming over?"

"Yep, and she's bringing Steve. Should I call Camilla over too?"

"Hell no. They aren't gonna be tearing our place up fighting. It's bad enough I have to try not to beat Steve's ass for this shit."

By the time Steve and Hailey arrived, my slight headache subsided. Ian stayed in the corner of the house furthest away from the entrance. As soon as Ian saw Steve, he clenched his teeth and balled his fists together while they rested at his side. I had to rub his back to calm him every once and a while.

"First of all, I want to apologize for bringing you two in this," Hailey offered.

"What about you, Steve?" Ian interrupted Hailey and overlapped her apology.

"Uh, yeah, me too. It was all just a big misunderstanding," Steve said.

"No," I jumped in. "Let's call it what it was. It was a big-ass lie. Why would you tell her something like *that*, Steve? You jeopardized not only your relationship with Hailey, but you compromised our friendship and nearly damaged me and Ian's. Not to mention your friendship with Ian! Camilla is also my friend. I mean, what in the world were you thinking?"

"He wasn't," Hailey said.

"Can I speak?" Steve chimed in. "I mean, I'd like to talk."

"Go ahead," I said as I fanned my hand in his direction giving him the okay to proceed.

"Okay, now Ian knew about me and Camilla before I even mentioned anything. So I knew he wouldn't think anything of it if I said I got with Josephine. But I figured Josephine and Hailey were such good friends that you two would be able to work it out and get over it."

"No!" Hailey and I both said together.

"No Steve!" Hailey yelled. "No woman . . . oh, no, not one woman wants to see her man with someone else — especially a best friend. What the hell is wrong with you? You make me sick right now! We have been through this bullshit before. Why are you with me? Because I walk around oblivious to our relationship? Like I'm happy with everything when deep down I'm not? Because I don't pressure you to get married when I want to bring it up every single week? Huh? What? What is it because I don't have a clue!"

Steve sat unresponsive as we all looked at him awaiting his answer to Hailey's burning question. My eyes darted around to everyone before returning my gaze back at Steve. Ian, who remained in the kitchen far away from Steve, sat with his arms crossed while he eagerly anticipated Steve's reply.

"Because I'm stupid," Steve finally said softly after he stared downward for a long while.

Ian sat back in his seat and put his hands on top of his head. I blew off Steve's revelation while Hailey nodded her head emphatically.

"Ya, think?" she replied. "Well, then you gotta work on that. But you know what? You have to work on that with someone else. I've had enough." Hailey stood to her feet and looked at me. "Can you take me home, Josephine?"

I looked surprised for a moment before I spoke. "Oh, uh, yeah, I guess so."

"I'll be getting my things out of your place this weekend, Steve. I'd appreciate it if you weren't there. Maybe you can go crash at Camilla's."

"Well, hold on," I jumped out of my chair and placed my hand on Hailey's shoulder and gave her a knowing glance. "Now Steve said it was a one-time thing and so did Camilla. She was angry with her man and she just wanted to get even or feel like she was getting even. That's all."

"Hmmphf!" Hailey blurted with attitude.

"Alright, let's go, Hailey . . . now." I pulled her toward the door. I turned back and looked at Ian, who still had one of his fists balled up. "Babe?"

He turned to look in my direction.

"You gonna be okay?"

He nodded and pressed his lips together. I knew he wanted to choke the life out of Steve and I hoped that when I returned I wouldn't see Steve's cold, lifeless body lying on the floor of our kitchen.

"Babe?" I asked again, apprehensively.

"I'm fine, baby. Just hurry back."

As Hailey and I hopped into my car, she barely waited for me to turn the key to the ignition before tearing into me with her frustration regarding this whole cheating situation.

"Josephine, did you know Camilla was seeing Bryan?" she asked me.

"Uh, yes. But I didn't know you were until the other day."

Hailey shook her head in disbelief. "I can't believe this crap. Camilla had both of my men? That fuckin' tramp."

"Wait, Hailey! Camilla didn't know Steve. And you didn't know she was seeing Bryan. She sure as heck didn't know you were seeing Bryan too. It seems to me that Bryan and Steve are to blame. But, you know, you and Camilla aren't victims either."

"Oh, so you judging me now?"

"No, I'm not. I'm just saying you can only be but so upset with Camilla."

"Whatever, Josephine."

"Hey, don't get upset with me. I'm an innocent bystander and your man threw me up in this mess. Ian was pissed at me after he saw you in the grocery store telling him that crazy crap. So that was why you weren't taking my calls? 'Cause you thought I was the one that slept with Steve?"

She huffed loudly and then nodded. "Of course, girl! Would you want to talk to you after hearing something like that?"

"Hell yeah, so I could find out what was going on! Hailey, you should know me better than that, really."

Hailey sighed again and then stared out of the passenger side window. She shook her head slowly and placed a comforting hand across her forehead as her elbow rested on the car doorframe. She tucked in her bottom lip to keep it from quivering. Suddenly, she began sobbing. Her shoulders shook as she sniffed softly to herself. Tears streamed down her cheeks as she decided to let them run instead of whisking them away.

"Oh, Hailey," I patted her shoulder. "I'm sorry about all of this."

She inhaled deeply, nodded to acknowledge my sentiments and wiped her eyes. She cleared her throat before she spoke and swallowed the remaining tears.

"You know, I knew it was going to happen again," she finally said. "It's what he does. It's all Steve does! That's why I wanted to be with someone else . . . to help desensitize me to his foolishness."

"I get that, but you can't use someone as a buffer to help deal with this. Have you told Steve exactly how you felt?"

"Girl, yes," she admitted, "but I may as well have been talking to his funky shoes."

"So," I began with a labored sigh, "why are y'all together?"

Hailey couldn't respond. She just shrugged and shook her head. Apparently, it was something for her to begin to think about if she had not done so already.

On the way to her house, we approached a stoplight at a busy intersection. She peered over in my direction, but looked over my shoulder past me. I turned to see what she was so fascinated by at that moment. It was a bar.

"Hey, can we stop for a drink real quick? Over there." She pointed to this place called Cosmo's.

"Well, I guess so. Just let me find some place to park. I have to call Ian though."

"Sure. Keep him informed. That's what lovers do, huh?"

*   *   *   *

Ian sat at the opposite end of the table than Steve in hopes that it would deter him from pouncing on him and beating his brains out. Not many words were exchanged between the two guys. It was at that moment that Steve wondered if he should have left shortly, if not right after, Hailey and Josephine departed. On the other hand, he wanted to clear things up with Ian before the situation got any worse between them.

"How is everything?" Steve asked awkwardly.

"Cut the shit, man," Ian barked back. "I almost went off on Josephine tonight. What was that bullshit?"

"Which part?"

"All of it! But namely the part that involves my woman. Man, let me tell you, if you ever do that again I will fuckin' kill you, man. You know how long it took for me to find her?"

"Look, man, I understand how you feel—"

"Nah, you don't. You got yourself a decent woman and you don't even know how to treat her. Then you wanna mess up what I got?"

"I know I messed up. I really messed up. Hailey ain't gonna take me back. Not now."

"Do you want her back?"

"I love that girl, man. Of course I do."

"Then you better beg like you've never begged before and prepare to keep begging. She's gotta know she can trust you, man. Leave them chicken heads alone. What the hell's wrong with you?"

"I know. I didn't know what was going on with Hailey that weekend and Camilla came on so strong that I just figured what the hell?"

"And then you got busted. You said it wasn't even good sex. Was losing your girl worth *that*?"

Steve stared off in the distance and shook his head robotically as if he clearly had something else on his mind. He knew that if he really wanted Hailey back he would have to think outside of the box and come up with a spectacular scheme in order to do so. This wasn't the first time this happened and each time his excuses became more and more transparent. At some point Steve knew that Hailey may just eventually find her another man and Steve could not live with himself if she was in the arms of someone other than him.

"I just need to go on and propose to her," Steve said.

Ian shook his head and rubbed the back of his neck. "No, man. Not right now because she will not accept a proposal from you."

Steve looked confused. "Why not? That's what she wants."

"Yeah, man, but she wants you to do it out of love not because you're afraid of losing her. What kind of shit is that?"

"I'm gonna get her back, but I need your help. Look, I'm sorry for dragging y'all in it, but I need y'all to help me get her back. Can you?"

"I ain't got no money," Ian declared.

The two friends chuckled at Ian's comment. For the first time since that weekend, Steve was able to laugh about something. He was determined to get Hailey to take him back and would do whatever it took.

CHAPTER 24

Tamar was elated that she was now waking up and getting dressed along with Donovan instead of watching him prepare for his long day. She was able to pay a few bills from the signing bonus and she felt good about herself. The road ahead actually looked attractive, and she could see her life smoothing out as she got back into a routine. She was unable to prepare breakfast for Donovan like she normally did just months ago, but she made sure that there were cereal bars and a hot cup of coffee for him to grab on his way out of the house.

After Donovan dressed, he joined Tamar downstairs in the kitchen. She was pouring herself a cup of coffee and packing her briefcase. He stared at her for a moment to take in every inch of her feminine frame. He teased her by moaning at her when he walked by to retrieve the creamer from the refrigerator. She giggled in response and patted his shoulder as he passed her.

"You look good enough for me to call in sick today," he said.

"Well, this is my first day on the job, so I won't be calling in sick for a few months," she said with a wink of her eye.

"I understand that. Let's try to meet back here at seven each night or at least in DC. Can you swing that, working girl?" He approached her with his lips puckered for a kiss.

"Mmm, that sounds like a plan."

*   *   *   *

Tamar hated being the newbie, but it was something that she would have to get over soon in order to do the job that she was hired to do. While she was still at home waiting to begin work, she took the liberty of scouting out a few prospects to work with her. She wasn't concerned about not being paid for doing this work because she knew eventually she would be compensated. She wanted to avoid wasting her first few weeks of work scrambling to find the "near perfect" candidate. She narrowed it down to five people. She selected two men and three women who all received their degrees from different schools and who were diverse in age and race. She was confident that she selected a good bunch to choose from. She wanted to convince Celeste that she may need three people, but in order for Celeste to agree, Tamar would have to state one hell of a case.

When Tamar entered her office, she stopped at the threshold and looked around the room. She took it all in and smiled. She had a huge, cherry wood desk and two bookcases with six shelves and two, burgundy, leather, winged-back chairs that flanked the matching leather couch. The coffee table was cherry wood as well. There was a flat screen, plasma TV between the bookcases mounted above the miniature refrigerator that was stocked with soft drinks, juice and water.

Tamar walked further into her office and noticed a door that was just to the left of her desk. She turned the knob and gasped when she peeked inside. The marble floor shimmered when she flipped the light switch to illuminate the recessed lighting. The shower stall was trimmed in gold setting. She looked around and noticed that the commode was also trimmed with gold fixtures.

"My own bathroom," she whispered. She smiled as she continued to look around and in an instant her smile dissipated as she said, "Wait a second. Just how long do they expect me to be here in the evenings?"

There was a knock on her outer office door.

"Yoo hoo!" the voice called.

Tamar turned and walked in the direction of the voice. "Celeste! Hi."

"I see you are getting familiar with your settings, huh?"

"This is incredible."

"Oh, well, wait until you see mine!" Celeste said as she laughed extremely too loud. "Get settled. There are a few packets on your desk to read. When you're done, come grab me. I'm down the hall. Let's take a nice, long, working lunch and I'll give you the lowdown, okay?"

"Sounds great," Tamar responded with a smile.

"Welcome aboard!"

Tamar sat at her desk and gave herself a spin in her swiveled, high-backed chair. She decided to set those appointments with the five candidates for the following day if they were available.

This is going to be great, she thought to herself. Tamar finally felt in charge again.

*　　*　　*　　*

Later that morning, Celeste and Tamar had an early lunch to discuss the company and its business at B. Smith's at Union Station. In a way, Tamar was hoping that she would see someone from her old firm and hoped they would ask her where she was working at the moment. Cressman & Marshall Law Firm was one of the top firms on the East Coast. Whenever the name of the firm was mentioned, without a doubt, people knew. They were in an 18-story building and possessed the lease for 12 floors. Most of the lawyers who worked there graduated from Harvard and were extremely familiar with several facets of the law. Tamar was fortunate to be among such an esteemed caliber of professionals to say the least.

After they ordered their entrees, Celeste gave her the run down of the company in a bit more detail than she had at the interview.

"Cressman & Marshall handles several aspects of law and we also serve as sub-legal to other firms in the area and vice versa. Our main focus is defense, criminal, medical malpractice and corporate law. Other areas also include divorce, general practice and international law and that's just a few. Have you done defense before?"

"Yes, I've done pro bono work for the DA's office two years after I graduated law school. It was gratifying work. I learned a lot there."

"How did you get involved in corporate law?"

"Well, it sort of just fell in my lap. I worked at my previous law firm for four years. I sort of got the feeling that they didn't really know what to do with me. I had experience in general practice, divorce and criminal, but they were fully staffed. I'm sure they didn't want to lose me to the competition and decided to try me out on a corporate case. Our legal team won and I was lead counsel. So there you have it. I was put on another case, then another and before long two years passed. I was one of their best attorneys and I deserved to make partner, but I guess they didn't think so."

"Was that why you left?"

"Umm, yeah, it was."

Tamar obviously did not know Celeste well enough to tell her the real reason why she left her firm. It was unimportant at the moment and frankly it was none of Celeste's business. Besides, Tamar knew that Celeste and Donovan knew each other and she felt that it was inappropriate to talk to Celeste about Donovan in any fashion.

"Donovan told me that he was placed in the position that you wanted," Celeste said as she gave Tamar a knowing smirk.

Tamar was taken off guard by Celeste's statement and for once was at a loss for words for a few seconds. She chuckled and took a sip of her iced tea before she spoke.

"Why would he say that?"

"That's what happened, right?" Celeste asked.

Tamar was not about to go down this road with Celeste. She was unsure where this line of questioning would lead, but she decided to end it at that instance and leave no room for Celeste to interrogate her any further.

"Actually, that's not what happened. By the time Donovan got there my resignation was already turned in," Tamar lied. "His second day on the job was my last day. He wanted me to withdraw my resignation, but I declined."

"Really?" Celeste asked apprehensively as she sat back in her chair and folded her arms.

"Really," Tamar replied firmly. Based on Celeste's gesture, she wondered exactly what the hell else Donovan told her. Nevertheless, she hoped that her response would be interpreted by Celeste as a signal to change the subject. The fact that she lied to her new boss in no way phased her. To Tamar, Celeste was still a stranger and would remain that way until she proved that she could be trusted — and so far Celeste missed the mark drastically. Sure they would work together, but she wanted to keep her personal life, just that — personal. Besides, Tamar was now testing Celeste. She wondered how often she and Donovan talked and if she would hear about how and when she resigned again anytime soon and from whom. All she had to do now was wait. At the moment, she felt no need to mention this conversation to Donovan.

After a brief moment of silence Celeste took a sip of her chardonnay and responded.

"Interesting."

Tamar decided to ignore her comment so as to not arouse Celeste to commence in another round of meddling. On second thought, since Tamar was unable to hide behind any bullshit, she thought it would be a good idea to have a conversation with Donovan about this after all.

*   *   *   *

As they both agreed earlier that morning, Donovan and Tamar met at her house at seven that night. Tamar had a big day ahead of her tomorrow and wanted to get enough rest so that she would be up for the task of interviewing prospects. One thing that she promised herself before she started this new job was that she would not bring the office into her residence. Tonight would be the exception to the rule.

She wondered what Celeste had on her agenda as far as she and Donovan were concerned.

Donovan greeted Tamar with a kiss, as usual.

"How was your day?" Donovan asked as he rested his hands against the small of her back while they embraced.

"Good. My office looks better than yours," Tamar bragged with a smirk.

"Oh, so you just gonna rub it in my face, huh?"

"Yeah." Tamar turned away from Donovan, her back pressed against his chest. He kissed her neck and swayed her gently from side to side. "Speaking of rubbing things in people's faces—"

"What exactly are you gonna rub in my face?" Donovan moaned after his comment and pressed Tamar's hips into his midsection.

She giggled as he leaned over and kissed her neck again. "Not that," she said. "Well, at least not right now anyway."

Donovan smiled.

"Celeste sort of rubbed the fact that you were selected for my job at the old firm in my face today. How'd she know about that?"

"What?" Donovan asked. He turned Tamar around by slightly turning her hips toward him. He stepped backward a few steps and leaned against the wall opposite from her and crossed his arms. "What are you talking about?"

"She and I had lunch together today and she asked me why I left my last job. Correction, as a matter of fact, she told *me* why I left. How would she know that?"

Donovan replied without skipping a beat, "I told her."

"Why?"

"She asked."

"When you were hooking me up with the lead, did you tell her that we were together?" Tamar asked.

"No."

"Oh, because she didn't ask?" Tamar replied sarcastically.

"Yeah, and because I didn't want anything to interfere with you getting the job."

"Hmm."

Donovan sighed and went to sit down on the couch. He felt that this may be a long night, so he kicked off his shoes and loosened his tie.

"What does 'Hmm' mean?" he asked.

"Hmm means I don't want her in our personal business whether she asks or not."

Donovan rubbed his chin and the front of his neck. He licked his lips and bit down on the bottom of his lip as if he felt the need to stifle what he wanted to say. He clasped his hands together as he rested his elbows on his knees and dropped his head.

"Okay. Alright, Tamar," he finalized.

Tamar unzipped her skirt and allowed it to fall to her feet. She bent over to pick up the garment and walked slowly up the staircase. Donovan raised his head and looked up to watch her as she ascended the stairs. Along with the satin blouse she wore, she donned black, sheer bikinis and thigh-high stockings. Donovan noticed that she still wore her high heels as well. Instantly he became aroused and no longer wanted to continue the subject of Celeste that could potentially lead to a nasty argument. He wanted what he craved all day from Tamar. He wanted to go upstairs and have his way with her, but was discouraged by their conversation. He knew his woman and he knew that she wanted to be with him as much as he wanted to be with her. She gave him the go ahead by partially undressing for him. It was clear to him that he would have to be the aggressor in this instance.

Donovan removed his shirt knowing that the sight of his bare chest would entice Tamar. He unfastened the button to his pants and partially unzipped them. He trotted up the stairs behind her, confident that within the next twenty minutes they would be well into their lovemaking.

CHAPTER 25

Hailey wanted to call Bryan so badly to see how he was doing after Josephine and Camilla caught her at his house. She still felt as though she did nothing wrong for Bryan to cut her off. She was only guilty by association. He had not contacted her since that day and she longed for his touch now more than ever. Unable to wait for him to reach out to her, she decided to call him to just let him know that she wasn't upset about him putting her out of his house.

"Hello, Bryan?"

"Hailey?" Bryan's tone sent vibes of positive energy into the receiver as if he just discovered that she was alive after not speaking to her for years.

"Yeah, it's me," she gulped nervously before she spoke again. "I, uh, I just wanted to see how you were."

"I miss you too, Hailey. I really do."

Hailey smiled and clutched her heart to keep it from racing. She relaxed her shoulders and leaned her head backward and let out a gratifying sense of relief.

"I thought about what happened and I was wrong," he said. "Can I see you?"

"I want to see you too."

"I've never been to your place. Is it okay if we met there?"

Hailey thought for a moment before she answered. She was so used to sneaking around with Bryan that it didn't occur to her that she could now invite him to her place. It wasn't as if she was in a committed relationship anymore.

"You know, I don't see why not."

"It's okay?"

"Yes."

"Let's meet up tomorrow after work?" he suggested.

Hailey dropped her shoulders somewhat disappointedly. She was hoping that she could see him that night and was unsure if she could hold out for another 24 hours. She was so smitten with Bryan that she was willing to take what she could get at that point. She wanted to ask him about Camilla, but decided not to at the moment. Instead she suppressed her thoughts of him being with another woman and told him that she couldn't wait to see him.

It was funny that she thought very little of Steve compared to Bryan. She didn't quite understand why that was. She knew she still loved Steve, but he betrayed her one too many times and that was the final straw for her.

She wanted to pretend that their relationship never happened, but that was impossible. The two of them had made so many plans together that there were still things left for them to accomplish, but that was all over now.

What made Hailey the saddest was reminiscing over the things they planned to do, which would now never be seen through to fruition. It was as if their entire relationship was one big lie. She came to the realization that everything she dreamed about her and Steve was undeniably unattainable. To her, there was no need to ponder over what could have been with Steve. Odd as it may seem, the tough love that she inflicted upon herself is what gave her the strength to continue to move on to get past the hurt.

Hailey knew that she was in no position or state of mind to meet someone new. She wanted to be with someone familiar. The only other man that she had known physically since she had been in a relationship with Steve was Bryan. He would make her feel better, she knew he would.

"Okay," Hailey agreed. "We'll meet tomorrow after work. There is so much we have to talk about."

"I feel like such a heel!"

"Can we try to just forget about it?" Hailey suggested. "I was just as surprised as you."

"I can definitely do that, love," Bryan said confidently.

After Hailey confirmed her plans with Bryan for the next day, she decided to begin packing the rest of Steve's items for them to either be picked up or dumped with the rest of the garbage. Among some of his items, she came across a tattered, red, raffle ticket. On one side it ordered the holder of the stub to "Keep This Ticket." On the other side it had three blank lines for someone to scribble text on them if they desired. Along the width of the ticket were a series of numbers preceded by the letter "C." C93201555. The raffle ticket signified the first carnival she and Steve went to together. She was unsure why he kept the stub for so long until she remembered the story that accompanied it.

The two of them stood for twenty minutes waiting for the winners to be called to receive an all-expense-paid trip to Atlantic City. There were at least four other smaller prizes to be won and they turned up winning nothing. Hailey remembered what Steve told her when she was about to chuck the ticket into the garbage. He told her that even though they hadn't won anything that night, he still felt lucky to be there with her.

Steve wasn't one to gamble or play the state lottery, but he thought he would try his luck the following day. He decided to play the last four digits of the ticket number, as those were the ones that were being called at the raffle the evening before. As a result of Steve playing 1555, it won him enough money to take Hailey to Atlantic City that same weekend. They collectively chose not to gamble, but decided to spend time walking the Boardwalk, eat at the most expensive restaurants and stay at the snazziest hotel.

Hailey smiled when she thought about the memories the little, red stub rehashed. She held it in her hand as it rested on her lap and took a deep breath. She already finished packing his items for the evening. She tucked the red stub back into the rear of the drawer that she retrieved it from and closed the drawer of the delicate antique nightstand gingerly. Some memories were hard to erase.

CHAPTER 26

Tamar and Donovan basked in the sexual afterglow as they were wrapped under the covers that evening. After Tamar made her position about Celeste known to Donovan, he followed her upstairs and apologized. She accepted his apology and decided that she was going to settle in for the night. Much to her surprise, Donovan had plans for her that evening. He kissed her repeatedly and caressed her body for several minutes until she gave in to his desires. She knew she was fighting a losing battle because just the sight of Donovan turned her on instantly.

As Tamar lay cradled in Donovan's warm, muscular arms she thought to herself, *I don't want any shit on this job.* She let out a sigh of discomfort that stirred him.

"You okay?" he asked.

"Oh. Yeah, baby. You?"

"I'm real good." He snuggled her tighter into his chest. "I've been thinking though."

"Really?" she asked as she intertwined her fingers with his. "Thinking about what?"

"Why don't you move in with me?"

Tamar became deathly silent as his question slathered her ears. He lovingly caressed the back of her slender neck lightly with his lips.

"Move in? Don't you like visiting me at my house?"

Donovan chuckled softly at her comment. "You are so funny, babe. I do, it's comfortable here, but I thought about it a lot this past week. It doesn't make sense for us to pay two mortgages."

Tamar sat up and turned to face Donovan. His bedroom eyes opened slightly as he looked into hers. She rubbed his chest gently with her fingertips, which he enjoyed, before she spoke.

"Baby, I like my house."

Donovan laughed loudly and pulled her closer as he kissed her on the forehead. "Okay, so rent it out." He laughed some more until he noticed that Tamar was not.

She placed her hand on his cheek and rubbed where his dimple disappeared once his amusement subsided.

"What are you saying to me, Donovan?"

He kissed the palm of her hand. "I'm saying to you, Miss Tamar, that I want to be with you and I want us to live together. Let's take this to the next level . . . if that's okay with you. I know you like working and being independent, but I would like the chance to take care of you."

Tamar's eyes began to well up. She didn't want him to see her showing any sort of emotion regarding his proposition. She cared for him, but she felt that if she gave up her independence, the very thing that made her who she was, that she would have to say goodbye to a large part of herself for good. On the other hand, here was a wonderful, extremely gorgeous and stable man willing to care for her. It would be a tough decision for her, but she wasn't going to let the decision be *that* tough.

"What if it doesn't work?" she asked.

"Then we work harder."

"*Then* what if it doesn't work?"

Donovan chuckled again. "Then we dig in and work even harder. I'm not letting you go that easily, sweetheart. I love you."

Tamar couldn't keep the waterworks at bay any longer. As tears streamed down her cheeks, she whisked them away quickly with her fingertips.

"I'm not a quitter," she told him.

"And neither am I. That's why this is gonna work for us."

"Don't you think I should get settled at the job first though?"

"Baby, that is strictly up to you. I will take care of you either way."

Tamar struggled to maintain her composure and tenderly placed her hand upon her neck to keep the lump that beckoned an onslaught of tears harbored. Instead, it kept her from speaking, so she mouthed the words, "I love you too."

*   *   *   *

The next morning Tamar prepared breakfast for Donovan as they both got ready for work. He ate all of the cereal bars in one day, so she knew that solution for breakfast would not work anymore. As she whisked two eggs for him, she thought about their conversation and wondered what exactly she would have to do in preparation to rent her house. She poured the scrambled eggs into the warm pan to make his omelet. She wanted to meet someone who brought most of what she had, if not more, to the table in a relationship. Asking this of a mate, she knew someone would have to eventually move in with someone.

"Mornin', baby!" Donovan nearly yelled.

Tamar spun around toward the sound of Donovan's booming morning voice.

"You're mighty chipper this morning," she told him as she tilted her chin in his direction to prompt him to kiss her cheek.

"Hey, I'm alive, the birds are singing, I have a beautiful woman making me breakfast after making love to me and did I mention she was beautiful?" He kissed her again and finished buttoning his shirt.

Tamar folded the omelet and slid it onto a plate. "There you go. I gotta take care of the man I love, right? You eat that up and I'm gonna finish putting on my face."

"You don't need to," he said as he stuffed a huge forkful of omelet in his mouth.

Tamar looked over her shoulder and winked at him before heading upstairs to the bathroom. She gazed in the mirror for a moment and then looked around at the reflection of the bathroom. *This is a great bathroom*, she thought to herself. She squeezed her eyes together tightly and inhaled deeply. She stared at her reflection again and allowed the air to pass through her lips when she exhaled.

"I'm gonna miss this place."

CHAPTER 27

Hailey didn't want to make the evening out to be a big production. She just wanted to spend some time with Bryan, maybe talk about the incident and send him on his way. At least that was how the scenario played out in her mind. However, things always had a way of taking an unexpected turn when it was not anticipated. Needless to say, if sex was going to pop up on the agenda for the night then she was more than prepared for that as well. Not only did her body yearn to be held and touched, she truly missed Bryan.

He arrived around eight and brought along a small bouquet of flowers. It surprised Hailey because he had never done that before. He kissed her innocently on the cheek, another thing he had never done before, and stepped across the threshold. He looked around, taking in everything that Hailey used to decorate her home. It was his first time there and he wanted to savor the experience. They had been seeing each other for almost five months and not being invited to a woman's home by then was strange for him. He didn't think that

Hailey had something to hide and certainly did not want to pressure her, but he couldn't help but feel that he was being denied a part of her. Standing in her living room confirmed something within him. He thought perhaps now she was ready to move forward in the relationship. However, he, on the other hand, was unsure if *he* was completely ready.

"Hi, Bryan," Hailey said as she watched him walk into her home.

Her lights were dimmed while jazz played softly. Bryan took a seat on her couch and smiled at Hailey as she approached to join him. As soon as she sat down and made herself comfortable, he put his arm around her shoulder and pulled her closer to him.

"Hailey," he started, "I would like to sincerely apologize for throwing you out the other day. You did nothing wrong."

Hailey slightly nodded. "True, I didn't. I had no idea those two were coming over. I was just as surprised as you that day."

"I can only imagine what you must've thought of me."

"Well, it wasn't good," she offered. She shook her head to emphasize her feelings concerning her private thoughts about him during that time. She patted his knee and continued. "But, I know you're only human."

Bryan took her hand and began to caress it. "You aren't just saying that, are you?"

"No, Bryan. It's how I feel. I had a lot of time to think about things since we've been apart. There are some things I'd do differently and other things I'd keep the same."

Bryan pulled Hailey in for a long kiss. He rubbed her back as she melted in his arms. She wrapped her arm around him and caressed the deep trench in his back to tickle his spine. He repositioned himself so he could lie on top while her legs wrapped around his midsection. He once again kissed her deeply before his lips slowly made their way down her neck and to her chest. He slowly peeled away her loose-fitting, linen, button-down shirt to reveal the top of her breasts, which peeked above her bra. He smelled her fragrance and moaned as he softly kissed her flesh. She rolled her eyes around in ecstasy as she hungered for him to enter her. Before she became completely helpless to his touch, she patted him lightly on his shoulder and he ceased his light ravishing. He lifted his body up on his hands and looked down on her. She was buried in the cushions of the couch.

"Bryan?"

"Yes, my lovely Hailey?" he responded.

"Do you still see her?"

"Who?" he asked as he tried to catch his breath.

"Camilla. Do you still see Camilla?"

"What? Why would you ask me that?"

Dissatisfied with his response, Hailey lifted herself up to scoot back on the couch. Once she was settled, she leaned back so she could vertically look Bryan in the eye.

"I think a simple 'no' would've sufficed," Hailey stated.

Bryan sighed and sat on the couch correctly. He looked straight ahead for a moment at nothing in particular and then looked at Hailey, who was buttoning up her shirt. She folded her arms and crossed her legs. He placed his hand to his forehead, obviously frustrated that this issue was intervening with their night of lovemaking.

"It was Jacqueline, right? She had something to do with this, didn't she?"

Hailey displayed a puzzled expression before she turned to look at him. "Uh, you mean, *Josephine?* And she had something to do with what?"

"Hailey, the day I kicked you and your friends out, I had to drive Jacqueline back to Camilla's so she could get her car. When we arrived, Camilla wanted to talk, so I obliged. Very briefly we spoke. She apologized and said that she wanted to work things out, but I want to be with you."

"Uh huh. Does *she* know that you want to be with me?" Hailey asked. "It's very important that you not lie about this, Bryan. Does she know?"

"She does now," Bryan told her.

Bryan was used to having several women back to back for different durations throughout his life. Without question he was a serial monogamist, but never had he dated two women at once. He enjoyed the thrill of being constantly wanted and having sex readily at his disposal. Although he enjoyed the sex with Hailey much more than Camilla, Camilla was a great cook who was always available and she seldom challenged him when he showed up late, neglected to call, or missed a date. She was easy. She was labeled as a pushover who adored Bryan. He loved that. Often times he wished he could combine the two women to create that one perfect woman for him. Hailey was sophisticated and attractive without trying to be. She managed to turn Bryan's head in a room full of people and that was an occurrence that didn't happen often. She always kept him guessing. He loved that she offered him mystery with her romance, while still making him feel that he was needed by her. It kept their relationship exciting.

Hailey nodded to affirm Bryan's statement while she caressed his cheek. He lifted his hand to hers, kissed the inside of her palm and then used her hand to caress his face. She faced him and looked him directly in the eyes as she delicately squeezed his hand.

"So back to my original question . . . do you still see her?"

Bryan lied to get what he needed from Hailey that night. "Of course not. She's history."

Bryan climbed back in front of her and smothered her face with kisses like a puppy would a little child.

He didn't want to think about Camilla when he was with Hailey. The truth was he wanted to be with Hailey just as he had in the past, but he didn't want to completely end things with Camilla because she did whatever he wanted her to do and that went a long way with him. However, from Bryan's past dating experiences, he strongly felt as though Hailey hoarded a deep secret from him. This was the first time he had seen where she lived since they began dating almost five months ago.

A confident Hailey, now feeling as though she could believe that Bryan terminated his relationship with Camilla, began tickling his neck with the tip of her tongue. She rubbed his shoulders and down to his chest as she continued to kiss his neck and soothingly nibble on it. She unfastened his pants and shoved her hand down them to harden his nature with her touch. Her body was on fire as she burned with desire to please and to be pleased. She wanted to be taken by him on the couch right then. Bryan, being the traditional lover, felt more comfortable in the bedroom. He scooped her up from the couch and prepared to ascend the stairs to her bedroom to make love to her.

The doorbell rang.

Bryan stopped and turned toward the door with Hailey still cradled in his arms. Hailey, just as surprised as he, arched her back and came to attention as she too wondered who the hell was ringing her doorbell. She looked at her clock that was mounted on the mantle to check the time. It was still early, but rarely did she allow visitors to come over unannounced.

"Who could that be?" Bryan wondered aloud.

"I don't know. Ignore it."

Bryan decided to do just that, but the doorbell rang again, and again, and yet again, eventually followed by rapid and frantic knocks on the door.

"Perhaps you should answer," Bryan suggested as he carefully placed Hailey on her feet. He was puzzled by the person's sense of urgency on the other side.

"Okay, but, I have no idea who this is," she said as her disclaimer.

She checked the peephole and stared for a rather lengthy moment. Bryan shifted his weight from one foot to the other as he stood, his curiosity mounting. As she continued to stare, more knocks came, but this time the raps on the door were accompanied by a male voice.

"I know you're in there!" the voice from the other side said loudly, but rather calmly for the volume.

Hailey slowly opened the door and Steve let himself inside.

"Hey, baby," he said and leaned in to kiss her cheek, but she backed her face away slightly to avoid contact from his puckered lips. Steve didn't see Bryan until after Hailey humiliated him with her gesture.

"What's going on here, Hailey?" Steve asked her as he pointed at Bryan.

"Who is this?" Bryan asked.

"I'm her boyfriend!"

"Good, because I'm her *man*," Bryan replied with an arrogant swagger and calmly refastened his pants.

Steve noticed the gesture and clenched his teeth along with his fists.

"Wait. Don't I know your ass?" Steve thought for a moment. "Oh! You that silly reporter from *The Post* who thinks he's the shit."

Bryan crept forward a little closer to Steve. "Excuse me?"

Hailey moved in between the two men before anything tragic ensued. She seriously doubted that Bryan would get into a scuffle because he believed himself to be too classy for that. However, she knew Steve would not hesitate in the least to wipe up the floor with Bryan. With that in mind, she tried to push Steve back toward the door as he walked closer and closer toward Bryan.

"Go, Steve!" Hailey turned to face Bryan with her back still pressed firmly against Steve to keep him from charging at Bryan. "I'm sorry, Bryan. Steve is my *ex*-boyfriend. And certain privileges like dropping by unannounced are no longer granted."

Hailey turned back toward Steve who was saddened by her statement, but more crushed that only a few days had gone by and she already had another man in her home. He wondered what type of relationship they truly shared after all of those years. He no longer felt that cosmic connection with Hailey. However, he was still willing to try bonding again with her and he needed to make his position known.

"You know, Hailey," Steve began, "I told Ian I wasn't letting you go. I know I messed up, but I want you back. That thing with Camilla was nothing, baby."

"What? Camilla?" Bryan asked as he narrowed his eyes and walked even closer to Steve. "Did you say Camilla?"

"What I said is between me and Hailey."

"How do you know Camilla?"

By now, Hailey was looking down. She pinched the bridge of her nose kind of hard, hoping she was just dreaming. She huffed loudly and sauntered to the couch. She flopped down on it, reached for the remote to her stereo and turned off the low-playing jazz music. She decided to just kick back while they discovered exactly how they were linked. She wondered why Bryan would even care, especially since he just told her that he was no longer seeing Camilla. She thought maybe Bryan was just territorial. Nonetheless, it was clear to her at that time that she would not be having sex with Bryan Bryant since Steve crashed the party.

After Bryan and Steve exchanged verbal notes about Camilla, which didn't take an excessive amount of time, Bryan walked over to Hailey, bent down to kiss her and told her he would talk to her later.

"Wait! You're leaving?" Hailey inquired.

"Yes, dear. Let's get together later this week, shall we?"

"Are you okay?" she asked him, concerned that Steve's visit would be used as an excuse to never see her again. She certainly didn't want that.

"I'm fine," Bryan lied. "It seems you two have some things to discuss and I owe you at least that much before you dump him. Again."

Steve, who was casually leaning against the wall, interjected rather loudly. "You better get your ass outta here, man! Hailey isn't going anywhere!"

Bryan brushed off Steve's tough guy attitude. "Right, of course. Hailey, we will talk."

With that, Bryan left. Hailey dropped her shoulders, obviously disappointed that the no frills evening she planned, that she thought would lead to dynamite sex, was now ruined. She stood and headed to the door to show Steve out, but he blocked her way and walked toward the couch instead. She began stepping backward from Steve's gait until she flopped down on the couch.

"What?" Hailey asked.

Steve took a seat next to her. After he ignored her question, they sat in silence for a moment. He was angry with her, but didn't want to argue with her. He had questions, but didn't know which ones to ask first. He pondered what just occurred and felt as though his future was being stripped from him before his very eyes. He cleared his throat to indicate that he was about to say something. Hailey sat at attention to receive the explanation that he should be prepared to give her for sending her friend away. Steve sighed heavily and took Hailey's hand. She snatched it away and stood over him.

"You have to go. We are not together anymore. You made your choice!"

"And it was a mistake!"

"It's ALWAYS a mistake. Always! Can't you understand I'm done, Steve?"

"No! Dammit, Hailey!" he shut his eyes tight before he lowered his head.

He lifted it and looked Hailey in her eyes. Sadly, he noticed that something wasn't there anymore. That spark that she once had that could ignite a roaring flame in his heart was gone. He decided to ignore the vibes that he received from Hailey and continued to plead his case.

"I know you still love me, Hailey. I know I messed up, but I want another chance to prove myself to you," Steve pleaded as he tried to reach for her hands again, but she lifted them out of his reach.

"No!" she yelled. "Another chance? For what? Another chance, another mistake. 'I messed up yet again, Hailey.' Steve, I'm sick of the excuses, I'm sick of the lies. No. I don't want it anymore. The only thing we have to show for the years we've been together is just that — years."

"So if there was no one else, if dude wasn't even in the picture, you still wouldn't take me back?"

She shook her head from side to side.

"Wait," Steve decided to ask again for clarification, "if you were here all alone right now, no man, no feeling for anyone else, you wouldn't take me back?"

"No!" she said sternly. "Why is that so hard for you to believe?"

"Because you still love me, that's why!"

"Wow, someone had a nice helping of arrogance this morning," Hailey noted. "Steve, I'm done. Enough is enough."

He knelt in front of her. She sat back further on the couch and folded her arms. She really didn't want him touching her, but she was not about to start a shoving match with him just because he was violating her space. She told herself that he would be gone soon because there was nothing that he could say or do to change her mind about how she felt toward him.

"So, you're saying you don't love me anymore?"

Hailey threw her eyes to the ceiling and let out a huge sigh that was finalized by a frustrated grunt.

"Just look me in the eyes and say it!" Steve demanded.

"I don't need to do that!" Hailey told him. "For what? So you can have closure? So you can forever remember me saying it when you replay it over and over in your mind? What is the point of doing that? I've moved on!"

"In three days? You've moved on?"

Hailey chuckled a bit. "Something like that. But you know what, that doesn't matter anymore."

"So why did you let me in tonight knowing he was in here?"

"Steve! You were banging on my door and ringing the doorbell like a fucking lunatic! What did you expect?"

Steve got up and sat next to her again on the couch. He placed his hand on her leg, but she lifted his hand gently and placed it carefully in his lap.

"Pardon me," she added for clarity.

"Oh, so now you don't want me touching you?"

Hailey sighed again, looked at Steve and spoke very calmly. "Steve, what exactly do you want? Why are you here tonight?"

"I told you, I'm not letting you go. I'm sorry. I'm so sorry that I did that to you. I swear I will do whatever it takes to win you back."

"What you aren't getting is that it's over," she told him. She held her hands straight out in front of her, crossed them and separated them to emphasize they were finished. "It's over. Finito, kaput, the end, no mas, done. There, I said it in four languages."

Steve reached for her hand yet again, this time she allowed him to take it because she knew that he would never get another chance to hold them after tonight. He gulped hard before asking her another question. Steve began to break out into a light sweat over the possibility of what her answer may be. His mouth became dry and his legs felt like a huge gelatinous mass melting as a direct result of his body temperature rising. He took a deep breath and tried to focus.

"Hailey," he started, "do you love that cat?"

"Yes!" Hailey shouted without hesitation.

Steve sat back on the couch for a moment to let that sink in. He bit down on his lip and tried to keep his composure. His chest heaved up and down rapidly and he felt like screaming at the top of his lungs, but he suppressed the urge to do so. He covered his face with both of his hands and put his head between his knees. He couldn't believe his ears. Hailey had been cheating on him for who knows how long. He realized then that she had given up on them a while ago. He was convinced there was nothing more he could do. He unleashed a silent barrage of tears behind his hands that shielded his face. He loved her and her admission to loving another man shattered him completely. The only thing that stopped him from wanting to squeeze the air supply out of her body by gripping her frail neck was the love he still had for her. It was strange, but it was true.

Steve learned a valuable lesson that night. He learned that loving someone meant putting her happiness before your own and Steve seldom practiced that. He knew this time was the breaking point for Hailey. Steve had no more fight left in him and he was out of ideas on how to even begin to make her fall in love with him again. Possibly what may have been his one ally,

Josephine, would more than likely be unwilling to help him with Hailey because of the lie he told on her. He was out of options. He lost the one person that he loved. He had no choice but to do the only thing someone in love with another person could do who wanted to be set free. He had to let her go.

He wiped his eyes, which Hailey did not attempt to sympathize with his hurt, and sat frozen on the edge of her couch for a moment. He looked at Hailey, who was sitting next to him with her arms folded as she glanced at the clock.

Yes, he thought to himself, *I lost her.*

He slowly stood to his feet and began walking toward her front door. He drug his feet as he walked, too tired to lift them, and placed his hand on the knob for a moment. As he stood at the door waiting to let himself out he silently prayed that she would stop him from leaving maybe to at least say that they could still be friends or leave some other opening for him to return back into her life. When nothing was said, he opened the door and let himself out.

CHAPTER 28

Ian and I had been to three different jewelers in the area so far this week and I did not see anything that I liked at all. Today, we began our search again and visited two more. I'm sure any single woman who believed in love would probably trade places with me right now, but I'm honestly getting a bit frustrated by this whole process. If the ring shopping is wearing me out in a week, what on earth will the wedding planning be like? Now granted, I saw several rings that had different things that I liked about them, but not a single one jumped out at me enough for me to yell, *"Ian, this is the one!"*

To hell with this! I was tired and hungry and I know Ian had to have been bored outta his mind. How did I know? Well, by the time we drove to the third store, he lagged behind me, almost stopping in his tracks because I wasn't racing to get through the doors of the jeweler's myself. The big tip off was when he began looking at watches. Maybe he isn't exhausted from going store to store, but perhaps he is having second thoughts about this whole "marriage" thing.

"Baby, let's go. My feet are killing me," I finally confessed.

"Okay. You want me to go get the car?" He was carefully removing the fifth watch he tried on while I was tasked with finding the perfect ring.

"Sure," I told him.

He darted out of the store and disappeared around the corner. I thought this may be a perfect opportunity to ask the male jeweler what he thought about the situation. I startled him because he just sprayed Windex on the glass case and prepared to sop it up with a paper towel.

"Okay, so this is our third store. He's not even looking at the rings anymore, but at the watches. What does that mean? You have 30 seconds before he pulls up with the car. Go!"

The jeweler took a moment to digest what I just said before he asked, "Have you pressured him about marriage?"

"No. He suggested it."

Puzzled by my response, the jeweler searched for words. "Hmm, well, it could be a number of things. Maybe he is looking at watches as a hint to you as what he would like for a groom's gift from you. Or maybe he's just tired." The jeweler took a long and labored pause and then said, "Orrrrr . . ."

"Or what?" I asked.

The jeweler shook his head and tucked the Windex and roll of paper towels under the counter. "No, I don't know you well enough to say," he mustered.

I grabbed both lapels of his suit jacket and pulled his face close to mine. "Or what?"

The jeweler cleared his throat before he spoke. I, on the other hand, held my breath.

"He didn't mean it and is just going through the motions. Now can you let go of me please?"

I let out the breath that was restricted from exiting my lungs in one quick verbal exhale. I slowly removed my hands from the man's lapels and smoothed them over. In my peripheral, I noticed that Ian had the car parked just in front of the store entrance. I looked over and saw him fishing around in the glove compartment. This twerp of a jeweler didn't know what he was talking about. Ian wouldn't do that. He was too much of a straight shooter to involve himself and anyone he cared about in elaborate games — especially one of such a serious nature.

"I apologize for grabbing you," I told the jeweler and then walked slowly out of the door.

I flopped down in the bucket seat of Ian's car and slammed the door shut. I folded my arms and stared straight ahead for a moment before I realized I needed to fasten my seatbelt. Once the belt was secured, I crossed my arms again and slightly poked out my bottom lip.

Ian ignored everything. He didn't even say anything about me slamming his door.

"Where do you wanna go grab something to eat, babe?" he asked.

"Ian, are you having second thoughts?" I blurted.

He was shuffling through a stack of loose cd's when he responded. "Second thoughts about what?"

"Marriage."

Ian looked at me and dropped the cd's in his lap. "What?"

"Are you having second thoughts about marrying me?" I repeated.

He chuckled and stuffed the cd's back into the glove compartment. After he slammed the door shut to the compartment, he placed his hand on my knee and gently squeezed.

"Are you crazy, baby? Why would you think that?"

"Because you were looking at watches."

He put the car into gear and slowly drove away from the jeweler's, still chuckling to himself. "Is that a crime? Baby, *you* didn't even want to go in there. You think I don't know my future wife? I know you, girl. I know your dogs are barking and that you're probably craving some seafood."

Now I started laughing. "I did have a taste for some crab legs." I laughed again and then mumbled to myself, "That stupid jeweler. I should've known better."

"What's that?"

"Nothing, baby. Let's go eat."

*   *   *   *

When we arrived at the restaurant and ordered our meals, Ian wanted to know if I had spoken to Hailey since the past weekend. I had no intention of contacting her after we had gone out for drinks at Cosmos because I wanted to give her some time to deal with the situation on her own. Besides, when we were at the bar, I felt like somewhat of a lush because I ordered my usual B52, but she ordered ginger ale!

Naturally, I'm prematurely assuming that she and Steve were able to work things out like the mature couple they have hopefully grown to become. However, this is Steve's second, maybe even third infidelity offense toward Hailey. I'm sure at this point she is frustrated with his repeated behavior and perhaps has even run out of ideas on how to keep their relationship progressing. As far as Ian's inquiry goes, it seems as though whenever he asks or thinks about Hailey and Steve, he automatically assumes that he and I need to reevaluate our relationship. I was not about to fall into that trap over dinner, so when he asked had I spoke to Hailey since the weekend, I simply told him the truth.

"No."

However, my response was not enough to satisfy his inquisition.

"Have you tried to call her?"

"No."

"What's wrong? You're not still upset with her, are you?"

"No," I responded. "And I wasn't upset with her. I was more so upset with Steve for lying on me."

"Oh. I was just wondering why you were being so abrupt," Ian asked as he sipped his glass of water that was overloaded with ice chips.

"Because, Ian, whenever you bring up Steve and Hailey, it's an intro to something you want to ask about me and us," I said as I unfolded my napkin and placed it carefully in my lap.

"Not necessarily."

"Okay," I agreed with him and then turned my attention to the oil paintings that towered over the patrons of the restaurant.

"Oh, I know you don't believe that." Ian stated with a slight smirk.

"I'm not saying anything else," I informed him with a chuckle.

We sat in silence for a while and sipped our beverages. On occasion he cleared his throat and I drummed my nails over the tabletop. He wasn't fooling me in the least. He was so smart in the car on the way to the restaurant and nailed the fact that I was craving seafood and claiming to know his future wife. He did not think that I knew my future husband? I decided to talk about something totally unrelated instead. However, I knew that there was something on his mind regarding us.

"Did you see all of the lovely paintings that are hanging?" I asked as I pointed upward.

Ian followed my finger with his eyes to see which painting I was directing his attention to. "Yeah, those are off the hook. They are huge! Can you imagine if we had one in our townhouse? We probably couldn't get it through the front door. We would just have to leave it outside on the deck propped up against the side of the house."

"Right," I laughed along with him. "Or knock out a wall and have it replaced with the painting — sideways of course."

"You are funny, Jos'. Just…," he started and then stopped himself from speaking.

"Just what?" I asked, with a bit of concern.

He stared into his glass of water, lifted it, and swirled its contents gently before he spoke. "Just if you ever think of going to someone else, please tell me. Let me fix it between us first, okay?"

He used his free hand to caress mine. I pulled my hand free and gently slapped one of his. Stunned, he looked into my eyes, completely bewildered by the gesture.

"See? I knew it!" I triumphantly scorned him. "I knew it was coming. You said that because of Steve and Hailey!"

"No, I didn't."

"Ian?" I shook my head at his naïveté and folded my arms. My lips pursed tightly together as I tried to avoid smiling.

"Whateva, girl. Alright, alright, you busted me! You happy?"

"See there? You are not slick. I know you, babe!"

The waiter came over to the table, his arms overloaded with our steaming entrees. He set my dish down in front of me, and then Ian's before he told us to enjoy our meals.

"So what do you think will happen between them?" I asked since he seemed to have a close friendship with Steve.

"I told Steve that if he really wanted her back, he needed to beg and keep begging, and then beg some more. So if he spent all weekend begging, she should take his beggin'-ass back."

"Oh, you haven't spoken to him?"

"No, I already told him what to do. Bastard pissed me off, but I'll get over it."

"Well, I'm sure they probably made up and are back together again."

Ian and I had complete confidence in Steve and Hailey's relationship no matter how rocky it appeared at the moment. They endured the worst and remained together despite the circumstances. Perhaps now since Hailey threatened to move her items out of his house and demanded that he do the same, maybe Steve will get his act together for good this time.

Little did we know the things that would unfold over the next few weeks.

CHAPTER 29

Tamar was now settled into her new job and successfully hired two new staff members to work with her. She attempted to point out the pros and cons of having three members, but Celeste told her that it was not in the budget. Tamar spent several late evenings getting the two newest employees up to speed and was confident in their abilities. Leah and Brandon were two sharp law graduates, each four years out of school. They would surely prove to be great assets to Cressman & Marshall as long as they didn't begin dating one another. She feared that they may become attracted to one another if they were not already. If she needed to, she would discourage it in the workplace, but for now she saw no need to interfere. Besides, she had to tend to her own relationship. She decided to stay with Donovan for the time being because he lived a bit closer to the city than she. It may not matter to most in other areas, but in DC, living fifteen minutes closer to the job could make a major difference in regards to the length of the commute to and from work.

Celeste came into Tamar's office without knocking and sat across from her desk. She stopped typing when she noticed Celeste and made herself smile. Normally, she welcomed the interruption, but at that particular moment she was right in the middle of a thought while she constructed a letter to one of the CEO's of a large firm that she and her team would be representing in a fraud case.

Without asking if this was a bad time, Celeste began dumping information into Tamar's ears.

"Okay, so we have this new case coming up. He is the owner of the huge fast food chain Beefy Burger. His name is Jamison Hedley."

Tamar let out a quiet sigh and leaned back in her chair. This sounded as if it was going to be a long story.

"Okay," Tamar said, urging her to get to the point.

"Two high school students get in a fight at one of his stores. Aside from the fact that one kid got the proverbial crap kicked out of him, he is deciding to sue Beefy Burger."

"Why?"

"One of the bonehead workers failed to clean up the floor from a previous patron who spilled orange soda. The losing kid fell backward, giving the opponent leverage. The opponent mounts the guy and beats him to a pulp. The clumsy kid ends up in the hospital with a fractured cheekbone, broken nose and ruptured spleen. It seems the boy kicked him while he was down too."

"So the kid, knowing he won't be able to get a dime from the kid who actually put him in the hospital, is suing Beefy Burger for not mopping its own floor?"

"You got it."

"What is he suing for? Med expenses?" Tamar asked Celeste.

"I think the 1.2 million that he's asking for will cover med expenses, college tuition and a new house for his poor, little mama and then some."

"Is he for real?" Tamar asked. "What firm is representing him?"

"The Law Offices of Vanterpool & Coleman," Celeste says while fanning her hand in the air to indicate that they are no big deal.

"I see. So when are we expecting Mr. Hedley?"

"He will be here to see you in another half hour," Celeste informed Tamar. "Do you have any questions?"

"You have his file?"

"Joyce is finalizing it now."

"Has he been sued before?"

"Many have tried, but few have succeeded. The one thing about this guy is his corporation and every chain of Beefy Burger has a huge booklet of policies, procedures and standards. He told me over the phone that his policy states that the floors and bathrooms are to be mopped every half an hour. Of course they have done studies to prove why every half hour is the most effective method. However, as I told him, when there is a spill there should be immediate attention to the spill, which may be the angle the plaintiff will take. But it was pretty crowded that day. He prefers to settle out of court quietly, but I don't think this kid has a case. You have a lot of work to do."

"Right," Tamar flatly agreed.

Celeste sashayed out of Tamar's office with a bit of arrogance in her stride. Tamar attempted to finish the letter that she was drafting for the CEO, but had completely lost her train of thought. She reclined in her chair and swiveled it toward the window so she could take a moment to clear her thoughts. She looked out and down toward Connecticut Avenue. There was construction taking place at which she smirked. They destroyed her favorite sushi bar to make room for some clothing store.

Tamar's intercom blared. "Ms. Livingston?"

"Yes," Tamar responded.

"Mr. Hedley is here to see you."

"Please bring him in," Tamar instructed. "Thank you."

Honestly, Tamar did not know what to expect of the owner of the Beefy Burger empire. Every week it seemed a new Beefy Burger sprang up. Gladly, there were none in the area of DC where Tamar worked. She hated their fries anyway. He was probably some stubby, balding guy that gained a large stomach over the years, who laughed at all of his own jokes like Elmer Fudd.

"Ms. Livingston?" the voice said.

Tamar thought she would swoon and fall out of her swiveling chair. Mr. Hedley was in no way how she pictured him. He was maybe late 40s early 50s, in excellent shape for someone who stood at about six feet. His salt and peppered hair was cut short to match the accompanying mustache and beard that shown prominently against his dark skin. He wore a dark gray, Armani suit over his crisp, white shirt and cobalt blue necktie. She hoped that her mouth was not agape when he first walked into her office, but she could not help but to acknowledge privately how handsome this man was.

"I'm Ms. Livingston," Tamar said as she stood to shake his hand.

"This is a nice office," he said as he shook her hand and took a seat across from her desk. "It has a lot of personality. I can tell that you are a hard worker. I like that."

"Well, thank you, Mr. Hedley," Tamar accepted his compliment.

"No, none of that. My father is Mr. Hedley. Please call me Jamison." He smiled and it lit up the entire room.

"Okay, Jamison. You can call me Tamar since we are keeping the pleasantries informal."

"Great!" he boomed. "So I'm sure Ms. Bacon gave you some of the details regarding my case?"

"Yes, she shared them with me a few moments ago. She also informed me that you want to settle out of court?"

"Yes. 1.2 million is a bit ridiculous. I was thinking maybe forty grand and a life time Beefy Burger Platinum Membership, which entitles him to a free meal once a week." He chuckled and his eyes sparkled.

"Well, that sounds wonderful, but in his eyes forty thousand is a far cry from being a 16-year-old millionaire."

Jamison looked at Tamar seriously for a moment, his smile slowly fading.

"However," Tamar started, "you may not have to do either. I believe you have a good shot at winning this case. Perhaps even have a counter claim or even get those two to do some community service for you."

Jamison began sparkling again with his smile.

"Well, don't get too excited just yet. We have to think of an angle of defense. I'm going to need a copy of all of your policies, procedures, etcetera. Do you have any video surveillance? And I will also need a list of names and numbers of your staff that worked during the time of the incident. Also, if you have any customers who dined in that paid with debit or credit cards, we can perhaps track them down and get a statement."

Jamison smiled again at Tamar. He rubbed his palms together and sat back in his seat.

"You *do* know what you are doing," he noted. "Is there anything else you may need?"

"That should be fine for now."

"Okay," he said as he stood. "It was more than a pleasure meeting you, Ms. Livingston."

*   *   *   *

Tamar had already broken her pact with Donovan about being home by seven. Several evenings, Tamar came home around eight or eight thirty at night. Fortunately on this evening, she got home by the agreed upon time of seven, but Donovan was not there like he typically was. Normally, if he were late, he would call her and vice versa. She had not heard anything from him as of yet. She decided to wait around the house for another half an hour or so and then contact him to see how much longer he would be. She was getting a bit hungry and had not taken anything out of the freezer to prepare for their dinner. She had no idea that she would be home by seven, but she was able to complete a lot of tasks today despite the impromptu meeting with Mr. Hedley. It also helped now that she had Leah and Brandon working with her. Tamar was pleased that they picked up the routine of the firm as well as knew how to prep and check cases fairly quickly.

After waiting about forty minutes, Tamar decided to call Donovan's cell phone. It rang and then went to voicemail. She tried him at the office and after three rings his voicemail was triggered. The recording of Donovan's voice urged the caller to leave a message, which Tamar ignored.

"I'll go get us some take-out then," she said aloud to herself as she hung up the phone.

Tamar drove to one of Donovan's favorite Thai restaurants and decided to order his favorite dish. When she arrived she placed her order and waited in the front of the restaurant to be called once it was prepared. *There were quite a few people dining that evening for it to be a Tuesday*, she thought, but, *on the other hand, the food was indeed quite good.* She paced the foyer of the restaurant and tried not to be in the way of the incoming patrons when she looked at the entrance of another popular restaurant. She walked closer to the windowpane and squinted to make sure she wasn't imagining things.

When Tamar saw him place his hand on the small of her back, she left the restaurant that she was in and crossed the street to visit the other.

Tamar arrived at the other restaurant and looked around the entrance. When she saw no sign of them, she figured they must have had reservations. She could feel her adrenalin being pumped faster through her veins. She didn't want to jump to conclusions, but felt she may have to in this instance. She searched the restaurant with her eyes scanning every nook and cranny. The hostess asked her twice if she needed help, but she was too focused on her search to even comprehend what the hostess said.

Finally, she spotted them. She decided to watch for a moment before approaching. Celeste caressed

Donovan's face as he smiled bashfully. He grabbed her hand from his face and kissed the back of it before he gently rubbed it and placed it delicately on the table. That was all Tamar needed to see. She stormed her way over to them, knocking a waitress off balance in her stampede.

"Hey, Donovan!"

He was stunned for a moment, but remained calm. "Baby, what are you doing here?" Donovan stood to kiss her on the cheek, but Tamar moved her face away from him.

Tamar tried not to raise her voice, but was unsuccessful as she felt several pairs of eyes on the trio. "What are you doing here? What the hell is this?"

"Oh, we just came out for a bite to eat," Celeste flatly informed Tamar with a wave of her hand to indicate that their rendezvous meant nothing.

"Am I talking to you?" Tamar asked her.

Celeste, feeling snubbed by the abruptness, cocked her head to one side and folded her arms. She then gave a knowing look to Donovan.

Donovan stood and tried to escort Tamar out. "Um, let's talk outside," he said.

Tamar ripped her arm out of his grasp and grabbed a chair from the nearest table. "Oh, no. You man enough to have her rub on your face and to bring her in here, be man enough to tell me what's going on . . . *in here!*"

"Nothing, honey. We are grabbing a bite to eat."

"No! That's what she said. Donovan, do not . . . I was across the street buying dinner for you and me! And you're up in here with . . . oooh, Jesus, help me right now!" Tamar clapped her hands together once loudly. She took a moment and tried to calm herself down. "How long has this been going on?"

"How long has what—" Donovan tried to ask, but Tamar slapped his face extremely hard.

"Tamar, you need to calm down!" Celeste yelled. "This is not the time nor place!"

Tamar looked at Celeste with her eyes narrowed. She took a moment and thought to herself, *Just do it.* She slapped Celeste too — even harder than she had Donovan. Celeste's chair reared back from the amount of force that Tamar welded behind that slap. Tamar stood, placed her hands on the table and moved her face towards Donovan's, their noses almost touching. She looked him deep in the eyes and spoke through gritted teeth.

"You two enjoy your meal."

Tamar stormed out and every person in the restaurant followed her with their eyes. The staff that stood between Tamar and the exit parted the way to let her through to the front door. Celeste placed a soothing hand to the side of her face. Donovan could not see Tamar once she made her way to the front of the restaurant, but he was able to hear her loud and clear when Tamar yelled, "Son of a bitch!"

"I'm leaving, Celeste," Donovan told her. "I knew this was a bad idea." Donovan, his face still stinging, tossed a few twenties on the table and left.

*   *   *   *

Tamar raced home, unsure as to how she even got there, and stormed into her house. After she flung the door open and threw her purse toward the direction of the living room, she slammed the front door shut. She kicked off her shoes, leaving them in the foyer and dashed upstairs.

She was not one to destroy other people's things, but she just wanted Donovan's items out of her house. She began thumbing through the closet and ripped several of his clothes off of the hangers. As she tossed his clothes blindly over her shoulder, they made a pile in the middle of the floor. His shoes soon followed in the closet ejection. She paused for a moment and headed for the phone.

"Hello?" she began. "I need my locks changed . . . as soon as you can get here . . .$85? No problem. See you in a few."

Tamar was never one to go back on her instincts or question her feelings. When something did not seem or look right to her, she always trusted herself. If all else failed, she at least knew that she could trust herself before anyone else. When a relationship was over, Tamar kept things moving and never looked back. She seldom entertained explanations and elaborate apologies, which always seemed to be the case with the men she dated who could not accept "no" as her final answer. She was thankful that she had the ability to move on from a failed relationship, with or without closure, and she allowed time to herself before jumping into another one. She knew what she would and would not tolerate in a relationship and infidelity was number one on her list of things that she unequivocally could not accept.

Once Tamar was done purging her closets of all things *Donovan*, her next room to tackle was the bathroom. The shaving creams, colognes, toothpastes, waterpik — it all would be thrown in a plastic grocery bag. She would double it of course.

"Bastard," she murmured as she tossed his special mouthwash into the bag.

Donovan's teeth were sparkling white all thanks to this particular brand of mouthwash that he swore by. He had a great smile and Tamar was always attracted to him, but today he was the ugliest man alive to her. Although she knew things were over with him, she had no idea how work would be tomorrow. She was determined to go into the office. She was not about to give Celeste the satisfaction of knowing that she aided in ruining her relationship with Donovan. She refused to be the person that called in sick just to mope around the house all day listening to love ballads, while stuffing her face full of junk food. Tamar's creed that she lived by was whatever people expected her to do, she made it a point to do the exact opposite. With that, she would go into work tomorrow, smile, work hard, have lunch, make calls, meet with clients and then take her ass home.

Tamar was almost looking forward to Celeste having the gumption to come into her office and threaten to suspend her, or worse, fire her. She meant to slap the hell out of Celeste tonight, and felt she deserved it. One instance has nothing to do with the other. It was an occurrence that happened off site and after hours and she would not be apologizing for her actions. Not only would the grounds for termination not be plausible, Celeste was flirting with and possibly screwing her man for who knows how long!

With the bathroom now being eliminated of Donovan's toiletries, the next stop was the kitchen. Tamar was fair. She would return everything that belonged to him unscathed as long as he accepted to take them and never bother her again. If he refused, she would simply tote them to the garbage.

As she descended the stairs, the front door opened. She stopped in her tracks about midway through her descent. It was Donovan.

"Tamar," he started as he tossed his keys onto the foyer table, "we need to talk about this."

"No, we don't."

Tamar did an about face on the stairwell and retreated to the bedroom. She had put his clothes in a lawn and leaf bag and his toiletries in a plastic bag. She grabbed them both and headed back downstairs. Donovan saw her toting the items and shook his head.

"We need to talk, babe," Donovan repeated.

"Do not call me babe and you have nothing to say to me!" She plopped the bags at his feet and walked into the kitchen.

Donovan followed her. "Tamar, if you would just listen," he pleaded.

Tamar turned to face Donovan, clearly frustrated with him and the whole situation.

"Listen to what? How you two have been seeing each other behind my back? That you were trying to rekindle some shit y'all had years and years ago? That you wanted her to keep an eye on me all day because you don't trust me, when you really don't trust yourself? What? Or do you want to share with me how well she makes love to you and understands you? Well, I don't need to hear it!"

"Tamar."

"And I for damn sure do not want to hear any lies about what I saw. It's over!"

Tamar continued into the kitchen and Donovan could hear her stacking and packing items. As he felt defeated, the only thing he could do was remain there, praying that she would change her mind. He was not used to this sort of behavior from women. He adored Tamar's strength, but he wanted another chance; one that Tamar clearly stated that she would not afford him.

For the first time in a long time, Donovan felt his heart breaking. He was positive that Tamar was the woman that he wanted. Nothing happened between Celeste and Donovan, but it seemed he would never have the opportunity to explain that to Tamar.

The fact of the matter was the two dated several years ago and talked about marriage. Unfortunately, the circumstances prevented that from occurring. Donovan had just started a new job at a law firm in New York and wanted Celeste to move to New York with him. Celeste was just getting her feet wet at her firm and was unwilling to relocate. They decided to end the relationship, but to remain in touch. When Donovan returned to the DC area, it would appear to any believer of fate that they were meant to be together. At the time, Celeste was in a stable relationship and Donovan never had trouble meeting and dating women. This had gone on for two years until Donovan met Tamar.

Donovan understood Tamar's anguish regarding her job and he wanted to make it up to her somehow. The only way he knew to rectify it was to ask his ex for a favor. He instructed Celeste to take good care of Tamar because she was a close friend of his. Celeste at the time had no idea Donovan and Tamar were dating and she obliged Donovan's request to hook his friend up with a job. When Celeste saw the two of them at the restaurant, she knew then that Donovan had used her to help his woman. By that time, Celeste's relationship had long since fizzled out and the old feelings she harbored for Donovan began to resurface.

Confused by the sudden attraction, Donovan wanted to be sure that his past feelings for Celeste would remain dormant. Celeste said her intentions for the evening were in fact to return to her place for a drink and a talk. Donovan of course knew better and figured the evening would end in sex. However, when they sat down at the table for dinner, Donovan knew that being there with Celeste was not right.

He could only think about Tamar and wanted to have her seated across from him instead of Celeste. Donovan knew then that Tamar was the woman that he wanted and needed in his life. If only Tamar could have heard the conversation they had just before she entered, she would not be asking him to leave her life.

Before Celeste caressed his face at the dinner table, Donovan told her that he was in love with Tamar and that this would not be happening anytime soon. While they were there, they would eat and chit-chat for a bit and then call it a night for the rest of their lives. Donovan instructed Celeste not to take out any personal vendettas for him out on Tamar in retaliation.

Tamar returned from the kitchen with yet another bag filled with Donovan's personal effects.

"Here," Tamar said has she handed it to him. "Bye."

"Tamar, you are wrong. Don't do this."

"I'm wrong? I'm wrong?"

"If you just let me explain!" Donovan raised his voice a bit.

"Do not raise your voice to me in my house! You have your own house, you can go back there and yell your head off. You have disrespected me. You tried to make a fool out of me by making that heifer work my ass to death so she could spend time with you. You just told me you guys went to law school together. When she first saw us having dinner in the restaurant is when you should've disclosed everything. I would've never taken that job if I knew that, Donovan. And I'm wrong?! Just get out!"

"Baby," Donovan started, "let me explain!"

"Please, Donovan, just go," Tamar held her hands up in surrender. "Don't worry about the key. I'm getting the locks changed."

Donovan paused for a moment, startled by her abruptness to end it all without him being able to defend himself. He shook his head, picked up the bags and started to leave.

"No," he declared before he dropped the bags at his feet.

He turned and faced Tamar, who had her arms folded in front of her, clearly disgruntled by his act of defiance. He approached her, gripped her arms and pulled her toward him for a long kiss. Tamar squirmed and wiggled as she tried to free herself, but Donovan was too strong for her. He pressed his lips harder against hers and refused to let her go. Once she stopped struggling to free herself, he gave her a more passionate kiss and slowly released her.

Tamar, now subdued, but still angered, stared at him while he stood in front of her.

"Tamar, I haven't been with Celeste since she and I broke up years ago," Donovan started. "No, I didn't tell her that you and I were seeing each other because I knew she could help you with a job and pay you well. I didn't tell you because I still felt bad about me getting your job. The truth is, I don't know too many people that could hook you up and pay you what you're worth. I wanted to help you, but you were being so damn proud!"

"Well, Donovan—"

"I'm not done!"

Tamar exhaled heavily and allowed him to continue.

"Right before you came over to the table, I told her that it was over. She wanted to be with me to try to reignite some old feelings, but there are none. I planned to eat dinner and that was it. Why do you think she sounded so nonchalant when you came to the table? She was upset with me for ending our friendship."

Tamar cast her eyes downward and thought about the explanation that he had given her. He reached for her hands and she looked up into his eyes.

"I love you, baby, but if you don't want to be with me, I have to respect that. But I'm gonna tell you right now, I'm not going to give up on us. I promised you that months ago and I meant it."

The doorbell rang.

Tamar freed her hands from Donovan's and answered the door.

"You called about changing a lock?" the service guy asked.

Tamar looked at the bags that were settled by the door. She looked back at Donovan and then to the locksmith.

"I'm sorry, but it won't be necessary."

CHAPTER 30

After work, I decided to head home and relax before Ian arrived. He said he wanted to get in a workout at the gym after leaving his job. Since I don't know how to boil a pot of water, I grabbed him something from a nearby restaurant for his dinner. I just wanted to pop a bag of popcorn and watch a chick flick before he got back. I had a little over an hour, so I could do it if I fast forward through the FBI warning, previews, opening credits and any parts that included excessive gazing into a lover's eyes.

After I nestled myself comfortably on the couch, my phone rang.

"Dammit, it never fails," I said out loud before I answered the call. "Hello?"

"It's me, I'm outside. Can I talk to you real quick?"

I knew there was no way now that I was going to get to watch my movie. It would have to wait until the weekend and even then I may not have a chance to view it. I set down the large bowl of popcorn and walked to the window to look outside. Sure enough, Camilla's car was parked in our driveway. I sighed as I walked back into the living room and used the remote to turn the film off.

"Come on up, Camilla," I told her and hung up the phone. I walked to the door and held it open until she got out of her car and made her way up the porch.

"Josephine, I'm sorry for just showing up like this!" she said as she walked inside and took a seat.

I closed the door behind her and followed her into the living room. After Camilla sat on the couch, she started crying. Baffled by her actions, I immediately consoled her.

"Camilla, what is going on? What's wrong?"

"Oh! Everything!"

I got up to get her some tissue and then sat back down beside her. "Okay, you're scaring me a bit. What happened?"

Camilla wiped her tears and quieted her crying. She pressed her lips together to deter herself from wailing with anguish. She clearly was not ready to speak, so instead, I tried to guess what was the matter.

"Is it your job?"

She shook her head.

"Is it your apartment? Your car?"

She shook her head again.

"Uhhhh, is it uh, your health?

She shook her head yet again as she dabbed the residual tears away.

Hoping that my next guess was wrong, I decided to take a shot in the dark anyway.

"Is it, Bryan?"

Camilla nodded. *Bingo!* I thought to myself. I wondered briefly what this guy did to hurt her feelings this time. He probably didn't return her silverware or drank all of her stock of red wine and burped in her face afterward. He was clearly not the man for her, but for some reason she could not ignore the feelings she had for him enough to move on to someone better, which is what she deserved.

"He broke up with you?" I continued to probe.

She shook her head again, however this time she took a deep breath and turned off the water works just long enough to tell me what was going on with her.

"Josephine, I'm pregnant."

"What?" I asked. "It's Bryan's?"

"I'm almost sure of it."

"Oh, no. Well, have you told him? Hold up. Wait a minute . . ." I paused. "What do you mean, you're *almost* sure of it?"

Camilla gathered her tissues and got up to toss them into the garbage. She sat down beside me on the couch and took another deep breath before speaking.

"That came out wrong. I'm pretty sure that it's his. I just don't know what to do. If I tell Bryan—"

"You mean, *when* you tell him, Camilla?" I quickly informed her.

"I'm scared, Josephine," she confided. "I'm afraid that if I tell him, he will walk out of my life forever. I wouldn't want this child if he did that. I know it's wrong to be selfish, but it's the truth."

"I take it you guys don't always use protection?"

"That's the odd thing. We do. There was one instance when the condom broke, but that was a few months ago."

"Well, how far along are ya?"

"Not far. Only about three weeks," Camilla sniffled. "I don't want this child."

I put my hand on her shoulder to try to offer some comfort, but it seemed as though she thought through this long and hard. For the first time in a long time, I was at a loss for words. I was certainly pro-life, but the harsh fact was that it was Camilla's body and her choice. She would have to make the decision by herself, but only after talking to Bryan.

"When are you going to talk to him?"

"I don't know. Honestly, I'm scared to."

"Why? He's not God!"

"I know," she retorted. "I just don't want him rejecting me."

"Camilla, it is a possibility. I'm sorry to have to say it, but it is. Would you like for me to be with you when you tell him if you're that scared?"

"I don't know," she shrugged. "I don't think he really likes you."

Just then, Ian entered with Hailey behind him. They were both laughing at something. My stomach sank to my lap. *Why, of all times, is Hailey here during this conversation?* I thought to myself.

I stood to greet her at the door, hoping she didn't see Camilla right away. "Hey, Hailey. You're looking cheerful."

"Yeah. Now that the baggage is gone! I saw Ian at the gym and he told me that you had been asking about me, so I decided to just come on over. I hope I'm not intruding."

Camilla peered toward the front by the entrance. When she noticed it was Hailey, she rolled her eyes and shook her head.

"Great," Camilla mumbled to herself.

"No, you're never intruding," I told Hailey. "However, now may not exactly be the best time." I tried to give a knowing look to Ian, who was gulping down Gatorade while he stood in his sweaty clothes. I never understood why he never showered at the gym. Ian, completely oblivious to what was unfolding, tossed the empty Gatorade bottle into the recycling bin and stood there while Hailey and I caught up.

"Uh, well," I started, "Camilla came over just before you guys got here."

"Are you serious?" Hailey sort of whispered, but she was heard by Camilla anyway.

"Yes," Camilla said as she stood up and walked toward the entrance. "I had to speak to Josephine. You know, she is my friend too."

"Okay, and?" Hailey replied.

"Uh-uh. We are not doing this," I interrupted. "Y'all please don't be mad at each other. You both didn't know. They kept you two a secret. Can we please all sit down and talk?" I extended my hand toward the living room to lead the way.

Camilla slowly walked back toward her seat while Hailey followed her. Hailey was sure to take a seat just opposite Camilla. Ian started toward the living room, but I stopped him by reaching for his arm.

"Uh, not you, Ian," I smiled and blew him a kiss. "Go wash."

Ian gave me a peck on the lips and whispered in my ear, "You better tell me everything that's said." He finalized his request with a kiss on the cheek and jogged upstairs.

I sat down with the girls and tried to smooth things over. "Hailey, I wanted to talk to you because I was wondering if you and Steve got back together."

Hailey glanced at Camilla uncomfortably for a moment before looking back at me. She cleared her throat and fiddled with her wristwatch. She decided not to answer that in the presence of Camilla. Camilla sensed the evasiveness from Hailey due to her presence and reassured Hailey.

"I don't want him," Camilla said.

Hailey smiled. "Well, that makes two of us."

"Hailey, you broke up with Steve?" I asked.

"Yes," she said, with no remorse at all in her reply. "Bryan and I are planning to be together. It's over between me and Steve."

Camilla inhaled deeply and reached for another tissue. She began quietly sobbing again. Hailey looked at Camilla rather strangely. Clearly she was unsure of why that bit of information would make her cry. I consoled Camilla again. Hailey was completely baffled and decided to speak as a result of her bewilderment.

"Okay," Hailey started, "why are you crying? What's going on here?"

"Hailey—" I tried to stop her.

"Do you still have feelings for Bryan?" Hailey continued. "It's over, dearie. He and I are together and there is nothing that is going to change that. Steve is finally out of the picture and so are you."

"Hailey, please!" I pleaded with her.

Camilla swam out of her whirling eddy of despair to respond to her comment. "Is that right?"

"Oh, that's right," Hailey confirmed.

"Oh, God," I said to myself.

"Didn't he tell you about me?" Camilla asked Hailey.

I perked up a bit at her comment as well. One minute she was afraid to talk to Bryan, now she had another story to tell? I hoped for the life of that arrogant bastard Bryan that he was not still seeing these two women! I shook my head as I tried to pat Camilla's hand in an attempt to persuade her not to say anything about what she told me to Hailey. I knew Hailey long enough to know that she was unprepared to handle Camilla's news.

"Y'all want something to drink?" I asked awkwardly.

"Tell me what?" Hailey asked.

"You just have to ask him," Camilla replied.

I knew that was not the answer that Hailey anticipated. No matter what happened, I was not going to let my two friends fight over some two-timing, double-dipping, heartbreaking man who has a ridiculous name!

"You brought it up! I'm asking you!"

"Talk to him!" Camilla affirmed. "I'm tired of being the only one being manipulated and lied to."

Hailey sat back for a moment, silent. She looked down in her lap and then apprehensively up at me. Just then, she jumped up and ran to the bathroom and slammed the door behind her.

"I hope she's in there bawlin' her freakin' eyes out," Camilla said.

I pulled about three tissues from the tissue box and threw them in Camilla's face. "I wish I wasn't in this. Both of y'all are my friends!" I got up to check on Hailey.

I tapped on the door lightly and called her name. "Hailey, it's me. Can you open the door?" I waited for a few moments and tried to hear what was going on behind the door. Unfortunately, the noise from the blades of the whirring fan inside the bathroom made it virtually impossible.

After a few more moments, the doorknob wiggled from the other side as the latch was unhitched. The door opened slightly and I slowly crept inside to find Hailey kneeling in front of the commode.

"Shut the door," she ordered me.

"What in the world? Are you okay?"

Hailey wiped her mouth with a few squares of toilet paper before she tossed it into the commode.

"I'm pregnant."

CHAPTER 31

It was ten thirty in the morning and Tamar hadn't seen a trace of Celeste all day. Tamar was not going to bother her and hoped that Celeste steered clear of her as well. She was still upset with Donovan and sent him home after he apologized. She informed him that it would probably be best if they cooled their jets on the relationship a bit because she was still unsure exactly what Celeste attempted to do. Although Tamar did not tell Donovan her intentions, she planned to watch every move he and Celeste made for the next however long until she was satisfied that Donovan was out of Celeste's system and vice versa.

The constant checking was what Tamar despised. It would have been easier for her to break things off with him and assume that he and Celeste were seeing each other. She could at least compartmentalize that. However, giving him a second chance and not knowing what could possibly be happening made her feel out of control. Instead, Donovan was forcing Tamar to trust him again. Given that task, she made it perfectly clear to him that he would have to earn her trust. He wanted to try to meet with her for lunch today, but she declined. She had too much work to do and did not want to jump back in with him feet first because he may see it as a sign of weakness, which she was far from being.

Tamar was reading over a deposition when she heard a knock on her office door. She looked up and saw that it was Celeste. She had with her two cups of coffee in a carrying tray. Tamar was unfazed by her presence, although she managed to repress the urge to haul off and slap her again.

"Yes?" Tamar asked.

"I wanted to talk to you," Celeste said. "Are you busy?"

"A little, but you can come in," Tamar told her, but pretended to continue to read the deposition.

Celeste entered and closed the door behind her. She walked slowly toward Tamar's desk and set the carrying tray on top of it. She sat down and quietly cleared her throat in preparation to speak. Tamar set the deposition down and looked at Celeste, awaiting her spiel.

"I bought you a cup of coffee," she said with a slight smile.

"Oh, no, thank you," Tamar responded. "What can I do for you?"

"Tamar, listen," Celeste began. "I'm sorry about what happened last night. I don't know what came over me."

Tamar could not hold back any longer. "You saw Donovan happy with another woman and, in a desperate attempt, you tried to steal him back for yourself. That's what came over you."

Celeste sighed and shifted in her seat. "Okay, I deserve that. Tamar, I admit, the way that Donovan and I split left the door open. I cannot deny the attraction that I still have for him."

"He's with someone else and you have to deal with that. And the way to deal with it is to find your own damn man. I never understood that about women who behave like you. Is it something that you have to prove to yourself? Some form of self-validation?"

"What we shared was wonderful, Tamar," Celeste tried to convince her.

"The operative word is shared, which is past tense," Tamar pointed out. "I'm not going to apologize for my behavior last night. What you did was selfish and petty. You should be grateful that all I did was slap you for trying to jeopardize what we have. It's over. He's moved on and you should too."

"You don't know that," Celeste slyly remarked.

"Oh, yes, I do," Tamar said as she lifted the deposition to begin reading it again, an obvious act of dismissal coupled with confidence.

"You know, Tamar, if I was really petty, I could bring you up on assault charges."

"You are petty, but you are not a dumbass. You're disturbing me while I'm working with something that is not work related. Now get out of my office, get out of my personal life and out of my face before I toss your desperate ass out of that window. And don't forget your tired-ass cups of coffee."

Tamar's intercom sounded.

"Ms. Livingston? Mr. Hedley is here to see you."

"Send him in, please," Tamar replied. "Now, Celeste, I'm sure you would not want your reputation besmirched over this. And there is a whole list of things I could pin on you regarding how and why I was hired. Don't go there with me."

Celeste narrowed her eyes at Tamar and tightened her jaws, resisting the urge to respond.

"If you'll excuse me, I have a client coming in now."

Tamar stared at Celeste quietly hoping that she would muster the audacity to even pursue some sort of legal battle. She would bury her, and Celeste being the savvy lawyer that she was, knew it. Even though Tamar signed a non-disclosure agreement with her former firm, Celeste often probed her for information and requested that Tamar share some of its practices. Prying for company information was completely against the law and Celeste could be disbarred for it if there was proof, which Tamar had plenty of. Emails, phone messages and text messages coupled with the fact that she made unfair demands of Tamar when she found out who she was dating. Celeste wouldn't stand a chance in court.

"I knew I did the right thing hiring you," Celeste told her. "You're smart, determined and professional."

"I'm all of those things and more. But I will beat a bitch down if need be," Tamar said with a smile.

There was a knock on the door and Mr. Hedley came inside without being invited in yet. Tamar figured that was just something that millionaires did; thought that they were entitled certain privileges that common folk were not.

"Tamar! How are you?" Jamison asked as he looked over at Celeste. He extended his hand to Tamar and acknowledged Celeste as well. "Ms. Bacon, how are you?"

"I'm great," she replied.

"She was just leaving. We were discussing an infidelity case. The other woman tried to threaten the wife, so to speak," Tamar masked.

"Oh, not good. The so-called other woman has no power," he added as he took a seat across from Tamar's desk. "We've seen enough movies and heard it plenty of times on these ridiculous talk shows. You would think the poor souls would get it by now."

"You'd be surprised," Tamar finalized. "Thank you, Celeste!"

Celeste narrowed her eyes at Tamar, picked up the tray that housed the two cups of coffee and quietly walked out.

"You know," Jamison started, "I'm glad you are working my case. Celeste is great, but you have a certain sophistication."

"I'm flattered, but she is a great attorney," Tamar mentioned as she accepted his compliment.

"Understandable. Nonetheless, I'm glad to be working with you."

"So what can I do for you? You know you're being billed for this time, so I hope it's good," Tamar said with a smile.

"Instead of calling, I wanted to stop by and get some information regarding my case. How is everything?"

"Not too bad. Now I spoke with the attorney representing Mr. Jeremy Douglas, the young man who's suing you, and laid it all out for him on the table. Mr. Haynes, his attorney, will confer with his client. My guess is they will drop the case and you'll just be responsible for my attorney's fees."

Jamison gave a single, hard nod, stood up and buttoned his suit jacket. "Sounds good," he told Tamar.

Tamar scanned his frame with her eyes. She just loved older men who took pride in their appearance as well as their health. She was sure he worked out, probably with a personal trainer to keep himself in tiptop shape. She looked at her wristwatch before she commented.

"Leaving so soon?"

"I was just in the area and wanted to stop by for a bit. I have another appointment in a few," he informed her with a smile.

"Okay, well, you're just past the quarter hour mark. I'll have to charge you for half an hour, Mr. Hedley," she slightly smiled back.

"Understood. Thanks for taking time out of your busy schedule to discuss business with an old man like me." He smiled and winked at her before leaving. Just before he let himself out, he walked back toward Tamar's desk and sat back down across from her. "Can we speak off the record?"

"You mean…for free?"

He chuckled to himself as he nodded. "Yes."

Tamar sat back comfortably in her chair and locked her fingers in front of her. She looked him intently in his eyes that were casted downward. His eyes met hers and he cleared his throat just before he spoke.

"I hope you don't think I'm being too forward, but are you seeing anyone?"

Tamar sat up and blushed. "Actually, yes, I am."

He shook his head as if he just missed the last train at the station for the night and would be stranded. "I knew it. I just thought I'd ask to be sure."

"And why do you ask?"

"Well, I didn't stop by to necessarily discuss my case. I wanted to see you again. I just had to know. Are you happy?"

"Yes," she answered.

"Doesn't sound very convincing and you don't seem to be happy with him, but okay."

"Well, I am. I was under the impression that you were married," she casually mentioned.

"Never been married. Still looking for someone special." He stood up again to end their verbal exchange. "I think you're extremely beautiful. If you ever want a change of pace, or if he treats you wrong, I hope you will think of me."

Tamar smiled at him, but did not comment.

He walked toward the door and said, "Have a good day, Ms. Livingston."

"Likewise, Mr. Hedley."

Tamar tried to get back to work, but found it extremely difficult. Jamison's scent still lingered in her office and her brain kept sending her flashbacks of his smile and the twinkle in his eyes. He may have sensed some displeasure with her relationship possibly because of what happened with Donovan last night. There was no way he could've read her that well. Tamar hoped that Celeste did not divulge any information to him prior to him coming to the law office. Nothing seemed safe for the moment. Tamar decided to stick to her original plan to wait and see how things unfolded over the next few months.

CHAPTER 32

Bryan Bryant decided to meet Camilla at her apartment to talk, as she requested. He was trying to solidify things now with Hailey and felt this meeting with Camilla would be a waste of time. Although he failed to break off the relationship with Camilla, he was slowly weaning her off and limiting the time he spent with her. He was a bit apprehensive about going to see Camilla, but when they talked over the phone she pleaded with him and refused to take no for an answer. He agreed and was determined not to lead her on in any manner while he was visiting.

Camilla made it a point not to do anything special for Bryan's arrival. For her, those days were over even though she still cared for him. She did not have any white wine chilling, or a tray of cubed cheeses, crackers or fresh fruit. She certainly had not prepared any gourmet dishes for him to feast upon either. Dressed plainly in a v-neck shirt and jeans, she sat and waited for him while she watched the local news. He was always late. Because of that, she told herself that he had 30 minutes from the agreed upon time to be there. If he was not there, she was going to leave without letting him know her whereabouts. It was somewhat paltry for her to act out in this way, but he needed to know that her time was just as valuable as his and should not be taken for granted.

The doorbell rang.

Camilla looked at her wristwatch. Much to her surprise, he was only five minutes late. *An improvement, but with a hidden agenda*, she thought to herself. She turned the TV off and answered the door.

Bryan stood there waiting to be invited inside her home.

"Hi," she said. "Come on in."

Bryan walked inside, somewhat awkwardly, as if Camilla were preparing to be interviewed by Bryan for an article in *The Post*. He sat down on her couch, leaving his jacket on to indicate that he would not be staying there for long. Camilla sat in a chair near him, which he thought was a bit odd.

"Why are you sitting over there?"

"Oh, it's comfortable," she responded with a smile.

"Sooo," he began, holding out the vowel of the word, "what can I do for you?" Bryan sounded like a loan officer in a prominent bank who was being annoyed by a vagrant from the wrong side of the tracks.

"A situation has come up and I wanted to let you know what was going on. That's all."

"Camilla, they have phones for this sort of thing."

"Well, this is not the sort of conversation that you have with someone over the phone."

Brian decided to remove his jacket and get a bit more comfortable. It seemed that this would take more than five minutes for him. He crossed his legs by lifting his right leg and placing that ankle on his left knee.

"I'm listening," he said.

"I've known you for about six months now and I know we've had a crazy relationship. In retrospect, I'm not even sure if I can call what we had a relationship. It seemed as if we saw each other when it was only convenient for you."

"I wouldn't necessarily say that, but okay."

"Anyway . . . some things have happened. We both were seeing other people. Well, *you* were seeing someone and I had a one night stand, which I'm not proud about." Camilla sighed and then stood up. She paced the floor just in front of Bryan nervously. Perturbed by her pacing, Bryan confusingly looked at Camilla.

"I'm certainly not proud about it, but it meant nothing to me," she continued to ramble. "I don't even talk to the guy anymore. You were seeing Hailey behind my back for God knows how long. Well, you were actually seeing the both of us, which is just wrong! I don't understand how men can do that and not even have a conscience about it. It's just crazy to me."

Just then Bryan interrupted her rant again.

"Okay, Camilla. What is this about?" His voice rose a bit.

"Bryan, I'm pregnant!"

Bryan stared at her for a moment. Camilla, frozen in her steps now, looked at him awaiting some sort of reaction. He scratched his temple, scoffed, uncrossed his legs and put on his jacket.

"Clearly, it's not mine."

"What?"

"You've had a one night stand that I know about. What about the others that I don't know about?"

"Excuse me?"

"I can't be responsible if you want to behave like a tramp. You being pregnant has nothing to do with me, period."

Camilla, knowing that he may say something to this effect, prepared herself for this response all week. She was done crying over the thought of him not wanting to be involved with her when she accepted the fact that he may relinquish all responsibility. Instead of being sad about it, she was stark raving mad at his response. She stood in front of him, toe to toe, and looked down on him while he sat on her couch. Bryan leaned back in the chair, unprepared for this action from Camilla.

"Now you wait a minute," she started with heaviness in her voice. "You are not going to walk out of here with some picture in your fragmented mind that I was running men in and out of here. Just because you treated me like some second-rate piece of ass does not mean that is what I am! I tried to do everything to be the woman you wanted me to be and you did nothing but treat me as if you were too good for me! You arrogant bastard! This child is yours and I don't need to be with you to know that it's yours, but you will face up to your responsibility after the shit you put me through. I will see to it if it takes me the rest of my life to do so! We're going to get a test and that's that. After the results prove that this baby's yours, you're gonna have to kick in. Do you understand me?"

"Now wait just one minute, Camilla!" Bryan tried to get loud with her, but Camilla interrupted him to verbally retaliate.

"I SAID DO YOU UNDERSTAND ME?" she screamed.

Shocked by the volume and intensity in Camilla's voice, Bryan looked up at her, whose hands where on both of her hips as her teeth were gritted. He slowly nodded in compliance.

"Now get out!"

Bryan slid over on the couch to get up because Camilla was not moving from her stance to let him up. He walked out backward for the sake of his own protection. He did not want to be stunned if she chose to throw a vase or other object at him while his back was turned. He put his hand on the doorknob once he reached it and gazed upon her, who was still clearly angry with him. He nodded again to indicate that he understood what she meant and he let himself out of her house.

After the few moments Camilla took to calm herself, she then covered her face with both of her hands. She slumped face forward on the couch and cried uncontrollably.

She reached for her cordless phone and dialed a number. When the voice on the other end answered, she began to speak. Her voice cracked from the flood of tears that just ceased momentarily.

"I just told him. He denied it and called me a few names...he just left."

*   *   *   *

Bryan drove home to his house in silence. He was in no mood for classical music or news radio. Normally, he would be preparing himself for the next book-signing event, but he was unable to focus on that at the moment. For some strange reason, he knew that Camilla called him over to her house to woo him and persuade him to reignite the small fire that he tried to keep alive with her. He was prepared to slowly break her heart yet again until she got the message without him outright telling her to leave him alone. She dropped some heavy and unexpected news on him.

Bryan potentially being a father would ruin his entire plans for his career path. Camilla's announcement was not what he anticipated at all. He wanted to be with

Hailey and was set to propose to her by the end of the year. They would be the newest "Who's Who?" of Washington DC and would jet set to all of his events and become well known throughout the nation. He was sure that with a woman like Hailey by his side, the sky was the limit. Now he had no clue what was in store for him over the horizon. He was sure that he was careful enough with Camilla so this sort of thing would not happen with her. The last thing he wanted was for her to be clinging to the relationship he cultivated with Hailey with her hand out every chance she got. Camilla made that clear tonight that she would make his life a living hell if he attempted to leave her out in the cold to raise a child by herself. He certainly was not about to tolerate that.

Hailey called Bryan earlier that day and told him that she had a surprise for him. She did not want him to be gone for too long because she was preparing dinner. Bryan tried to take solace in knowing that the exchange between he and Camilla could be forgotten for the moment while he was comforted by Hailey.

When he entered his house, he could smell the magnificent aromas of spices that were carefully used to season the main dish and the accompanying vegetables. He smiled as he tossed his jacket on the back of the oversized recliner that could easily fit two people before entering the kitchen.

Bryan stopped in his tracks when he saw the vision of his beloved Hailey. She was stirring something in one of his copper-bottomed pots while wearing one of his dress shirts with four-inch heels. She turned when she heard him come in and smiled widely at the sight of him. He approached her, wrapped his arms around her and laid a wet kiss on her lips.

"It smells marvelous in here," he complimented as he peered in one of the steaming pots, "and you look absolutely ravishing, Hailey."

"Why thank you," she said. "Tonight is a special occasion for us."

"Really?" he asked as he nuzzled her neck and placed his hands under the shirt that she wore.

"Why don't you get washed up and then we'll eat first, okay?" Hailey said as she wiggled away from his grasp.

"I won't be long. I promise you."

By the time Bryan came back, the table was prepared for him as the food still steamed from their plates. He took his rightful place at the head of the dinner table and she sat at the other end and watched him as he ate.

"Oh, my, Hailey. This is incredible."

"Thank you! Eat up, hon." Hailey began to eat her food in silence as she watched Bryan enjoy his meal.

As he consumed his food, Hailey thought it would be a good idea to ask him a few questions of her own. She dabbed her mouth with her napkin and sipped her chardonnay.

"So, Bryan, where'd you go before coming here?"

"What? I'm coming from work."

"Are you sure?"

"Why, yes, Hailey! Where else would I have gone?"

"You didn't stop off to see an old friend?"

"Hailey, please. End the mystery, dear. Of course not." He sipped his wine and nodded in approval then continued his meal. "Besides, what old friend would I even venture to see?"

"Camilla."

Bryan stopped eating and put his fork down. He wiped his mouth and quietly burped behind his balled fist before he spoke.

"Of course not. No."

"Okay, fine. If you want me to, I'll believe you."

Bryan flashed a relieved expression and sipped his chardonnay again to clear his pallet. He loosened his collar and began to sweat lightly. He took another bite of his food and could no longer enjoy it. He placed his fork down a bit clumsily as he tried to concentrate on what Hailey was saying to him even though his stomach did not feel too settled. His eyes were glazed over and he blinked hard once to focus.

"Are you okay?" Hailey asked him. She stood to console him if needed.

"Excuse me, dear," he mustered before he dashed to the bathroom.

He slammed the door shut and Hailey followed. She could overhear him regurgitating in the porcelain bowl. Hailey covered her mouth to keep from laughing as she leaned against the wall just opposite the bathroom. She could hear the toilet being flushed several times.

"*Uuhhhhh*," Bryan bellowed, his voice muffled by the closed door.

Hailey covered her mouth tighter as her shoulders shook from silent laughter.

Bryan opened the door and Hailey's fits of laughter were masked by looks of sheer concern and gentle kindness.

"Are you okay, baby?"

"You put something in my food?" Bryan accused, his speech considerably slurred.

"Bryan, why would I do that? What did you eat earlier today?" She patted his back gently.

When he failed to respond because he was wiping his mouth with a hand towel, she put her hands on her hips and asked him another question, but this one with a bit of attitude.

"Did you stop off somewhere to eat before you came home?"

"Hailey, I just want to lie down for a moment."

"Okay, lie down on the couch, why don't you?"

Bryan turned to look at her and fell backward on the couch. Instead of landing comfortably, he rolled off of the edge and hit the floor with a loud thud. Hailey giggled silently as she extended her hand to help him back up on the piece of furniture. He took her hand and lifted himself to the couch with her help. He stared at her in disbelief and smirked from embarrassment.

"Thank you, dear," he told her. "I just need to rest."

"Okay, I'll save my news for later. You rest up."

Hailey rubbed Bryan's forehead gently as she knelt beside him while he was lying on the couch. Bryan tried to smile through his physical anguish to let Hailey know he was a trooper. She unlaced his dress shoes and removed them from his feet so he could relax even more. After doing so, she tossed the light, cherry-colored, chenille throw over his legs. He laid there, eyes closed like a five-year old being nursed back to health so he could return to a rousing game of kickball with his friends. She lightly patted his knee and headed toward the kitchen.

Hailey couldn't help but hear Camilla's voice over and over when she called her just moments before Bryan came home. She did not want to believe that Bryan outright denied being the father of her child. Camilla sounded crushed, but as Hailey promised Josephine, herself and Camilla, they would not fight over Bryan Bryant any longer.

Hailey raked the uneaten food from Bryan's plate into the garbage and began to feel bad for lacing it with a few drops of ipecac. She just wanted him to experience her vomiting spells since finding out that she was pregnant, not to mention getting some payback for him still seeing Camilla behind her back. She was not proud of her actions in the least, but a small part of her gleamed with delight by the visual of him dashing to the bathroom. She decided that when she tells him the news about her pregnancy, she will also come clean about how and why he became sick to his stomach. Besides, she also wanted to know why he lied to her.

Hailey's cell phone rang while it was nestled in her purse. She went to retrieve it and did not recognize the number. Normally, she ignored calls from numbers that were foreign to her, but out of curiosity, she answered.

"Hello?"

"Hailey?" the voice asked.

Hailey smacked her lips and tossed her eyes upward. "Steve? What do you want?"

"You," he replied clearly.

"We've been down this road already," she explained.

"Hailey, I need to talk to you. I need you. I want you, baby. I'm sorry, but I can't live without you. Please, Hailey."

"You're begging."

"I know and I told you I would. I want you back! I messed up bad. Please, honey."

Silence.

"Hailey?"

"Steve, don't do this," Hailey began, trying not to give in to unleashing any tears. Her voice cracked as she continued. "Why are you calling me now?"

"Hailey, I need to see you. Please, baby. You know I love you."

"I'm sorry, I can't deal with this right now. I have to go."

"Hailey!"

At the moment Steve called out to her from the receiver, she closed her flip phone. She held it next to her chest and breathed in and out heavily. She threw her head back and tried to retain the verbal soundtrack that accompanied her tears by pressing her lips together. She wiped her tears away and sniffled before she tossed the phone into her purse. She turned to go to the living room to check on Bryan, but he was standing in front of her, which scared her profusely.

"Oh, my God, Bryan! I thought you were resting?" Hailey clutched her heart to contain her surprise.

"I was, but it sounded like you were having problems with the person on the phone. Who was that?"

"It was Steve," Hailey admitted.

"I thought you told me he stopped calling you?"

Hailey crossed her arms and immediately got defensive. "Just like I thought you told me that you stopped seeing Camilla?"

Bryan gulped hard, swallowing down what was sure to be a follow up to his first heave and tried to respond to Hailey's accusation. When he couldn't, he walked away and went back to the couch. Hailey followed him.

"Bryan! Don't walk away! Tell me the truth. Did you see her tonight?"

Bryan collapsed on the couch and Hailey sat next to him waiting for his response.

"Hailey, I went to see her because she said she needed to tell me something."

"She needed to tell you what?"

"It doesn't matter. It's over between me and her!"

"You told me that last month!"

"It is! It's over. Can we just move on? What is your news? Didn't you have some news for me?"

"Yes, I did, but I don't know if I should share it with you now," Hailey admitted as she wrung her hands nervously together.

"Please," he pleaded.

Hailey sighed and rubbed her stomach delicately. She placed a soothing hand on Bryan's knee before she spoke. He placed his hand over hers and mustered a slight smile.

"Bryan, I'm pregnant."

Bryan paused for a moment as he studied her face. He looked down at her stomach that only bulged ever so slightly and then he looked back into her eyes. He smiled and pressed his lips firmly against hers.

"This is wonderful, Hailey! I was going to wait until Christmas to propose to you, but why wait? Let's get married. This is the confirmation that I was waiting for. I love you, Hailey!" He held both of her hands gingerly as he spoke. "What can I get for you? Do you need anything?"

"Bryan?"

"You've made me so happy! Let's drive down to North Carolina so we can tell my folks. They are just going to love you!"

"Bryan!" Hailey stopped his tirade.

"Yes?"

Hailey placed her hand to her throat to deter the lump from forming that typically indicated when an ambush of tears was about to become apparent. She gagged slightly before she attempted to speak and then took a deep breath. She covered her mouth as her eyes welled up. Bryan comforted her by rubbing her arm gently.

"Bryan, I don't think this is your baby. There is a strong possibility that it could be Steve's."

CHAPTER 33

This was going to be my first time meeting Donovan. Tamar refused to tell me the whole story about what happened with them weeks ago because she wanted me to report any vibes I experienced from him. The only thing she told me was that they had an argument and were slowing the relationship down. I haven't a clue what the argument was about. Since Ian was not really the type to do the double date thing, I was flying solo again. The good thing was that I never felt like a third wheel, but at times I wished that Ian would take some of the pressure off of me. Unfortunately, it is not going to change or get better once we are married even though that is what married couples do — hang with other married couples, discuss how many times their children peed in the bed, and the idea of getting a new hypo-allergenic dog.

I arrived at the restaurant early and decided to order myself a B52 while I waited. I was unsure what Donovan looked like other than the description Tamar gave me. She told me that he would probably be the finest brother in the entire restaurant and would be wearing a suit. The only problem was her interpretation of fine was different from mine. However, I recognized an extremely handsome man anywhere. Based on the accolades that Tamar gave Donovan, he seemed to fall into the extremely handsome category.

While I sipped my drink and peered at the entrance of the restaurant occasionally, my cell phone rang. It was Tamar.

"Hey, girl," I answered. "Okay. So how late will you be? And just how am I supposed to entertain your man for half an hour? Damn, Tamar . . . okay, okay. Bye!"

I rolled my eyes and that warranted an apprehensive look from the bartender.

"You don't like your drink?" he asked.

I chuckled. "Oh, no. My friend is running late."

Just then a strikingly handsome man stepped to the bar and ordered a glass of Riesling. I looked him over and he was wearing a tailored suit. If I had to guess, and I'm poor at this kind of thing, I would say it was Italian. This had to be Donovan. I thought to myself, *Tamar did well for herself.* He's attractive, a lawyer, has his own home, no kids — she hit the jackpot. I decided to introduce myself to him.

"Hi, I'm Josephine. Tamar just called and said she's running a little late."

"Tamar?" the man responded.

"Yes. She said she would be here in about half an hour. She had a few briefs to finalize for her case in the morning. You must be Donovan." I extended my hand.

He smiled wide and accepted it. "Josephine, yes. How are you?"

"Good. Sorry Ian isn't here. He hates double dates. But if you're into sports or working out, I'm sure you'll be meeting him soon. I reserved a table for us. I'm just waiting."

"No problem. So what are you drinking there?"

"A B52. It's my old standby," I responded with a smile.

The gentleman caught the bartender's attention and pointed to my small glass. "Can you give this young lady another please?"

"Why thank you!" I said.

I was really proud of Tamar's choice. I loved her dearly, but she wasn't one for settling down too quickly. I was kind of surprised when she told me that they were quite close to moving in together. He seemed a bit older than she, but I suppose his sophistication and genuine nature overpowered the age difference.

He sipped his Riesling and smiled at me again before he spoke. "How do you know Tamar?"

"We used to work together a while back. I'm in advertising and she was one of the lawyers that worked there. We have similar taste in clothes, so we decided to take a lunch trip to the mall and have been friends ever since. I usually can't afford what she purchases, so I live vicariously through her wallet!" I laughed and so did he.

"She never told me she had such charming friends."

"Oh," I lightly hit his arm as if he were my brother. "Thank you so much! Now . . . do you dare to tell me how you two met?"

I gave a knowing glance before I sipped my drink. He snickered, sipped his Riesling and carefully set his glass down before he spoke.

"What did she tell you?"

"Oh, no, Donovan. You're not trapping me with that one. I'm embarrassed to even repeat it. You tell me in your words."

"Why don't I let Tamar retell the story when she gets here?"

At that moment, another well-dressed man came to the bar. I didn't really notice him at first, but I thought if Camilla weren't pregnant, I would suggest this place to her because the second guy was handsome as well. He looked around a bit and ordered a Jack and Coke. When the bartender delivered his drink, he sipped it and drummed his fingers on the bar as he looked around. I decided to get out of that man's business and continue entertaining Donovan as Tamar instructed me to do until she arrived.

The guy at the bar reached for his cell phone that was strapped to his belt. He dialed someone and waited for an answer.

"Yeah, babe. I don't see your friend. No. You said Josephine, right?"

When I heard my name, I instantly tuned out the sophisticated man to listen to the rest of the Jack and Coke drinker's conversation.

"So you really aren't going to tell me everything she told you about how we met?" the man asked me again.

"Uh, wait just a second," I held my hand up as a gentle gesture to excuse myself from our conversation. "Excuse me?" I asked the man who just arrived to the bar. He didn't hear me at first because he was still on the phone.

Puzzled that my attention was redirected elsewhere, the sophisticated man looked behind him at the guy who was on the phone. He smiled to himself and finished the last bit of his wine.

"Excuse me?" I asked the guy again, louder this time.

"Hold on, babe," he told the person on the other line. "Can I help you?"

"Are you Donovan?"

"Yes."

"I'm Josephine."

"Oh! Okay," he told me. He got back on the phone to end his conversation. "Baby, she's here. Okay. I'll see you when you get here."

"It was nice meeting you," the man told me before he tried to leave.

"Uh, excuse me? Wait a minute, sir." I lightly grabbed his arm to thwart off his retreat. He nervously cleared his throat and dropped his head as he smiled.

"What's going on?" the real Donovan asked me.

"This man told me he was you," I pointed at the mystery man and smiled a bit, somewhat curious as to exactly what this man's motives were. Eagerly anticipating his excuse, I folded my arms across my chest.

Donovan smiled, recognizing that the man was trying to run game on me, but I could sense he was anxious to see how this man was going to back peddle out of being caught in an intricate lie.

"Oh, really?"

"Yes, really. Do you mind telling me who you are, sir?" I asked him again.

"I'm sorry," he apologized. "My name is Jamison Hedley."

Donovan perked up with discovery. "You're the Burger tycoon?"

He nodded sheepishly as he looked down and then up into my eyes. He gave a slight tilt of the head and shrugged his shoulders.

"Sorry."

"Okay, why would a burger tycoon impersonate a nobody?" I pointed to Donovan. When I realized what I said and done, I gave Donovan an apologetic look before I added, "No offense."

"None taken," he responded as he tried not to laugh.

"I happen to know Tamar. I'm one of her clients actually."

"Really?" Donovan asked, obviously impressed. "She didn't tell me that."

"She is quite professional," Jamison stated as he put a few bills on the counter to pay for all of our drinks.

"But, why would you say you were him?" I asked again, obviously still baffled.

"When you are a tycoon, you do things to entertain yourself. I do apologize for deceiving you, but I certainly enjoyed our conversation. When you mentioned her name, I just couldn't resist."

"Well, you have to join us for dinner," Donovan said, "that's if you don't have any prior engagements."

"I'd love to. Josephine?" he asked, brandishing a puppy-dog-eyed expression.

I smiled and swiveled off of the barstool to stand. I grabbed my second drink, looked Jamison in the eye and shook my head before giving in.

"Alright. I hope Tamar doesn't mind and maybe she can get to the bottom of this. Besides, our table is now ready."

The hostess showed us to our seats and brought another chair for Tamar. There were still things that I wanted to know about Donovan, but felt it wouldn't be appropriate discussing his and Tamar's personal life in front of a client. While we waited, Jamison ordered a bottle of champagne for us. I hoped that he wasn't trying to buy our friendship. If this tycoon impersonates and deceives people for his own entertainment, there is no telling what else he was liable to do.

After we were settled in our seats, Jamison wanted to propose a toast. To what, I was unsure, but I decided to interrupt him before he began.

"Shouldn't we wait for Tamar?" I asked.

"We can get another bottle when she comes," Jamison answered and then lifted his glass higher. "Please . . ."

Donovan raised his glass as he waited for Jamison's toast.

"To good food and new friends!"

Donovan and I obliged by saying in unison, "Cheers."

Just as we gulped down our drinks, Tamar slowly approached the table. She gave Jamison a comprehensive gaze, which lacked expression. I was a bit tipsy, but not to the point of embarrassment. Since I had a nice buzz going, I did not realize that when Tamar was closer to our table, I instinctively, but quietly, clapped and cheered.

"She's here! Hey, girl!"

Both Donovan and Jamison stood until she sat down. Tamar leaned over to hug me as I sat in the chair. She kissed Donovan and sat down as he held her chair for her. However, she was still eyeing Jamison, puzzled that he was here.

"Mr. Hedley? What are you doing here?" she finally asked.

I poured her a glass of champagne while Jamison started to explain. He cleared his throat and loosened his tie.

"I was at the bar and Josephine thought that I was Donovan," he explained without further elaboration.

"And? What else?" I egged him on.

"And . . . when I heard she was waiting for Tamar, I ran with it and pretended to be Donovan. Then Donovan shows up later, I have egg on my face, they invited me, the Burger Tycoon, to join you all for dinner. I hope it's okay with you, Tamar. If not, I can leave."

Donovan awaited Tamar's reply. It was clear to me that Donovan saw Jamison as a great networking opportunity or maybe just as another person he could hang out and do rich "guy stuff" with. Either way, Donovan was impressed and wanted him to chill with them.

"Mr. Hedley, I can't believe you would dupe my friend and boyfriend. It's really up to them. And since they've already okayed it, I guess it's fine with me." Tamar tipped her glass toward him and sipped her champagne.

"So, Jamison," I began, "how did you end up being one of Tamar's clients?"

"It's a pesky little lawsuit that I'm trying to avoid. Two kids get in a scuffle in one of my chains and one fell. The one who fell is trying to say that he lost the fight because he slipped and fell on soda."

"That's what's wrong with America now," I interjected. "No one wants to take responsibility for their own actions. Had they not been fighting in the first place, he wouldn't have fell! That really bothers me about this generation coming up. What examples do they have? Not to take away from Tamar or Donovan because we need good lawyers like them, but there's nothing on TV except court shows. Even those poor soap operas are being viewed less and less."

"I admit, when Drucilla was on *Young and the Restless*, I used to check it out every day," Donovan admitted as he and I laughed.

The rest of the evening went off without a hitch. Jamison remained charming, and not to toot my own horn or anything, so did I. We polished off another bottle of champagne and shared enough food to feed a small village. At the end of the evening, Jamison insisted on paying for everything, but Donovan decided that they should split the bill provided they could go golfing together. Jamison agreed. I only wished Ian was here. Lots of times he misses out on some intricate details of my life and I have to retell them to him when I get home.

Perhaps he enjoyed that one-on-one time with me as I described my so-called adventures.

While we waited for Donovan to get his car, Jamison shook Tamar's hand and told her, "I can see why you two are together. He's a good man. Thanks for a classy evening."

Donovan pulled up and Jamison opened the door for Tamar. After she got in, he said his goodbyes to Donovan.

"My man!" he said. "It was great meeting you. Take care of this lovely lady. And I'll see you on the green next week!"

"You got it!" Donovan replied. "Thanks again!"

Jamison turned to me and extended his hand for me to lead the way to my vehicle.

"Thanks again for dinner and the drinks," I told him as we walked. "I had a great time."

"No problem. I hope I can do it again soon, lovely lady."

I blushed when he said that.

"Now I know I played a trick on you and for that I apologize. I wanted to talk to you when I first got there. Why'd you think I sat next to you at the bar? When I heard Tamar's name, I couldn't help myself. Now you can hold that over my head for a while, but it could also be a great story to tell our grandkids."

"Whoa!" I giggled. "Grandkids? I hardly know you. And I don't even eat at Beefy Burger, sir."

"I'm sure you don't with that figure. Okay, I won't pressure you, but, here, take my card. Think about it. I would like to see you again if that's okay with you. If not, I'll be heartbroken for at least the next 10 to 20 years or so."

"Where is your wife?"

He laughed. "Why does everyone think that I'm married? I'm not married. I never have been. I wanted to be for the longest, but it's not necessarily easy for me either."

I stared at him, a bit unconvinced as I smirked.

"Here," he said as he scribbled on the back of his card. " This is my home number, tag number, personal email . . . you want my social too? Heck, you can look on the internet and find out everything there is to know about me. I'm 46 and single. No kids. I am looking for someone special, but it's hard these days. You seem genuine to me. It seems all of the lovely ladies I meet are in relationships. I can see why Tamar is sticking with Donovan. But where is your man? He should've been here too."

"Okay, okay, enough of that," I said as we reached my car. "He has his faults just like everyone, but he's good to me."

"Think about it, Mrs. Hedley. I mean, Josephine," he smiled as he opened my car door.

I got in and tossed his card in my purse convinced that I would throw it away later when he wasn't around.

"Have a good evening," I told him.

"And you too, lovely lady," he said as he brandished a smile that must have cost a small fortune and gently closed the door. He began walking away.

I pulled out of my parking space, sighed loudly and drove home in silence.

*   *   *   *

When I arrived at home, Ian was watching some television show that I had never seen or heard of. He was reclined on the couch, one of his favorite resting places, wearing a black wife beater and black jogging pants. He had on sweat socks, which one of his toes poked through a moderate-sized hole. I grinned to myself and shook my head.

"Honey, I'm home!" I playfully yelled.

Ian sat up and looked in my direction. He smiled and stood up to greet me.

"Hey, baby. Did you have a good time?"

"Yes, and I would've had an even better time if you were there."

"You know that's not my thing, Jose," he said as he walked toward the kitchen. "I made you something. I'm not sure if you have room for it or not."

I followed him with my brows furrowed. "What is it?"

He reached in the fridge and handed me a small dessert dish. The contents looked like pale, yellowy custard.

"It's Bananas Foster," he nonchalantly informed me. "I made it while you were gone."

I stared at the dish a bit longer than necessary while he held it in his hand. I couldn't bring myself to accept it. Instead, I continued to stare at it and unintentionally began sobbing. His facial expression displayed bafflement with a twinge of curiosity as to why my emotions spiked so drastically from the time I came home to that particular moment.

"What is it, Josephine?" he said as he placed a comforting hand on my shoulder, his eyes brandishing the utmost concern.

"I love you so much," I confessed to him, trying not to choke on my own tears.

"I love you too, baby," he responded. He took the dessert and set it on the counter and then placed my hands in his. "Why are you crying? Did someone say something to you while you were out?"

"Ian," I said as I gathered myself, "I love you. It's the little things you do like making me little desserts and tossing your sweaty gym clothes on the floor and laughing at all of my corny jokes."

"Yeah, you are pretty corny."

"I can't wait to be your wife and have as many babies as our house can hold."

He looked down for a moment and then he rubbed his entire face with his hand from his forehead to his chin. He looked into my eyes for a moment and then he scanned the rest of my body.

"Stay right here," he said before leaving the kitchen.

A bit puzzled, I stood there and slowly turned around to see where he may have gone. I looked at the mini dessert and picked it up. I sniffed it and it smelled like fresh, ripe bananas and liqueur. I reached for my purse, which sat on the other end of the counter within arm's reach. I set down the dessert and dug around into my purse to retrieve the card that Jamison handed me earlier that evening. I read it and then tore it into four pieces and tossed it into the trash. I smiled to myself and kicked off my heels.

"You can leave those on," Ian instructed as he came up behind me. He lifted me by my waist and placed me on the counter.

"Ian—" I started.

"Shhhs . . ."

He slowly unfastened my blouse button by button. He peered beneath the silk fabric to get a glimpse of my breasts. My heart raced as I knew what I was about to be in store for. I leaned my head back as I closed my eyes in anticipation. I stared back down at him as he reached my last button and began gently pulling my shirt tail from the band of my skirt. He flung the opened panels of the shirt simultaneously away from my frame before he gave his instruction.

"Finish taking it off."

I complied with his request as I felt my folds moisten. After I practically tore my blouse off, unable to sustain myself from his sexual quest, he wrapped his hands around my waist and squeezed it before he unzipped my skirt. I leaned back against the wall while he began to shimmy my skirt past my hips.

"Oh, baby," he said as he looked at my caramel complexion wearing nothing but my white, lace bra and string-bikini underwear. He pulled off his black wife beater revealing his rippled stomach and bulging chest, which he tossed on top of my pile of clothes. He carefully removed my underwear and gave more instructions.

"Put your feet up here and slide down."

I did exactly as I was told. He began fingering me slowly and he leaned in for a long and wet kiss. With his free hand he ripped off his tear-away, warm-up pants and they gathered at his ankles. He kissed my swollen vulva and began licking it slowly with his tongue. I arched my back to show my pleasure, but he didn't venture there for long.

He lifted up and gently entered me. That first insertion felt so sweet that I almost had an orgasm. His rhythm leisurely increased with each stroke, he steadily looked me in my eyes and never blinked as if he were studying my face like it was art. I placed one of my hands to his cheek and caressed it, the other on his chest.

The more his strokes increased in speed, the higher my ecstasy peaked until I couldn't hold it any longer.

"Oh! Ian!"

"Yes, baby?" he said in the sweetest, yet, most masculine voice I'd heard him use in a long time. That sent me over the edge.

"Ooooo-woooo! Ian! I'm coming!" I yelled as I gripped his shoulders and shut my eyes tightly to prepare for the sonic boom that erupted in my loins. My orgasms came one after the other as he stroked deeper and deeper inside of me.

Thirty minutes into our lovemaking and Ian was still going for the gold. His strokes were out of control, almost animalistic as he pumped harder and faster. I knew it wouldn't be long before he joined me. He grinded the base of his penis against my clitoris in a circular motion while he sucked gently on my neck. That triggered more orgasms from me as I could feel my pelvis contract and pulsate on his manhood.

"Ah, baby. Mmm, Josephine. Damn that felt good!"

I tried to catch my breath and unsuccessfully ignored the subsequent set of orgasms that stirred in me as he continued to stroke over the next several minutes. As he neared his climax, his strokes became more vigorous as he pressed his sexy lips together.

"Ahhhhhh!" Ian moaned as I felt him release himself inside me. He collapsed tenderly onto my stomach and kissed it softly. "Oh, Josephine."

I caressed his forehead lightly with my fingertips and whisked away the tiny beads of sweat that formed from his sexual workout.

"Ian, baby," I started, "oh, my God."

"Can I lie like this for a second?" he asked, causing me to giggle.

"We can stay here all night if you want. The freezer's right there too. You can just reach in there for some ice when my butt gets numb."

He smiled, his eyes still closed, as he caught his breath. He moved his hands from my waist to firmly cup my breasts. I looked down at him and shook my head as I lightly chuckled. I gave him a few more minutes before I nudged him again.

"Hey, you? Come take a shower with me," I said to him.

$$* \quad * \quad * \quad *$$

After our hot shower, we dried ourselves off. We left the steamy bathroom to cool off and then wrapped ourselves into a blanket before cuddling up on the bed in each other's arms. With a soft light illuminating the room and the best of Sade playing softly, I couldn't help stroking his chest as it slowly rose and fell with each breath that he took.

"Hmmmm . . ."

"What was that?" he asked.

"What was what?"

"That sigh. What's on your mind, baby?"

"I'm just concerned about Hailey and Camilla." I tickled his chest with my fingertips as I spoke. "I think it's going to be a long pregnancy for both of them."

CHAPTER 34

Tamar and I decided to throw an intimate baby shower for Camilla and Hailey at the same time. I was pleased that the two of them were on speaking terms and actually became good friends throughout their pregnancies. They shared different experiences from being pregnant and spent several evenings crying on each other's shoulder. The relationship that cultivated between those two women may be odd to some, but it was necessary. After all, there was a strong possibility that their children could be siblings.

After everyone left the baby shower, the three of us decided to stay and chit-chat at Tamar's for a while longer and review what gifts were received — the good, the bad and the ugly. They had a pretty decent haul. Hailey was well into her ninth month and could be delivering any day. Camilla was about a month behind her. They were going to be having boys.

Everyone did pretty well that evening not mentioning Steve or Bryan, but Camilla was having a pretty rough time. She had me and Hailey, but received no sort of support from Bryan. Although she braced herself for this behavior from him several months ago, it still hurt her tremendously. Bryan had gone all out to prepare for him and Hailey's son's arrival. Just as he promised, he proposed to Hailey. Just as he assumed, his family loved Hailey, they were thrilled that he would be a father and they were happy that he would be settling down soon. Camilla tried not to let this bother her, but she often mentioned it to me. She admired Hailey, but still did not understand the extreme difference in emotion displayed by Bryan to the two of them. Whenever she brought it up to me, I would try to change the subject and focus on the new life she would bring into the world.

"That was a nice turnout," Tamar said. "Too bad y'all couldn't have any wine because there was a bottle that someone brought that was really good!"

"Yeah, but it won't be long now," Hailey mentioned as she tried to get comfortable on the couch. "I'll be sipping some again soon!"

"Yeah, in about 18 years!" Tamar teased her.

Camilla emerged from the bathroom and took a seat next to Hailey. "Oh, my God! That's the eighth time today!"

"And the day ain't over yet!" I reminded her. "So are you guys nervous?"

"Yes!" they both said in unison and then giggled.

"Well, you both look great for pregnant women," Tamar said. "I hope I'm that fortunate! No excess weight, no ankle swelling, you're both glowing and noses didn't spread across any faces."

"Gee, thanks!" Hailey said with a chuckle. "We both meet up and walk three days a week. It gives us a lot of time to swap stories and talk about, you know, other stuff."

"I'm proud of the both of you, really," I commented.

Camilla rubbed her stomach and looked a little sad, but mustered a smile for me and one for Hailey.

"It's hard some days, but I'm managing," she told us.

Just then Hailey leaned back and clutched the lower portion of her stomach. She let out a gust of air from her mouth as she said, "Whew!"

"Uh, attention . . . attention. . .," Tamar impersonated a voice on a loud speaker. "No deliveries will be accepted on my couch. Close it up and report to your nearest hospital."

We laughed at Tamar's joke, but Hailey didn't.

"Oh, hell!" I said.

*   *   *   *

We arrived at the hospital and called Hailey's obstetrician on the way there. Camilla had begun breathing heavily herself and we warned her not to go into labor as well. She was beginning to get overly nervous; I supposed anticipating the moment her time would come. Neither of us wanted to call Bryan to tell him that Hailey was about to deliver, but Tamar did the honors. He was just going to refer to me as Jacqueline again anyway. What a nut.

I stole a moment to call Ian, who said that he was going to call Steve. They were going to make their way to the hospital. I wasn't so sure if that would be a good idea since Bryan would be there, but when Ian called me back to tell me he was on his way, Steve insisted upon coming along. He assured Ian that he would "be cool."

Camilla, Tamar and I were in the waiting room when Bryan showed up. Camilla casted her eyes down and did not want to face him again. Bryan ignored her and asked which one of us was Tamar, which was a silly question. He knew me and obviously knew Camilla. Tamar stood to calm him. He extended his hand, but Tamar patted him on the back instead.

"She just went in," she told him. "It's been about half an hour."

"Where is she? Where's my fiancée?" he asked in a slight panic.

Camilla cringed at the sound of his question and rubbed her stomach in a circular motion. She rocked back and forth and breathed heavily, but Bryan ignored her. I sat next to her and patted her shoulder.

"Are you alright?" I asked.

She moaned a bit and nodded before she spoke. "Mm-hmm. I'll be fine," she whispered to me. "Tell Tamar to get his ass outta here. I'm suddenly feeling stressed. He's making my baby hurt."

I immediately did as instructed. I stood up and spoke quietly into Tamar's ear. She leaned in so she wouldn't miss a word.

"Tamar, can you take him to her? Like…now?"

"Uh, right. Follow me." Tamar summoned Bryan and walked away with him close on her heels.

"Uh-oh," Camilla said.

"What do you mean, 'uh-oh?'" I asked her as I slowly sat back down next to her.

Just then, Steve and Ian rounded the corner in such a hurry that they almost passed Camilla and me.

"Where is she?!" Steve yelled.

"Man, will you shut up?" Ian said. "We're in a hospital! Hell you yelling for?"

I got up to kiss Ian and greeted Steve with a hug. "Hey, Steve. Long time no see."

"I know. You look great. How long has she been in labor?"

"About half an hour or so. I think she will be delivering soon."

"I want to see her. God, I really want to see her."

"Now, Steve, you know what's-his-face is here. Don't cause a scene. He *is* her fiancé," I reminded him.

"Whatever," he said followed by a waved hand.

I looked over Steve's shoulder and saw Donovan casually making his way toward the waiting area. He was reading each sign as he passed. He was overly calm as he sauntered toward us. The only thing missing from his gait was him whistling a tune. I supposed since Tamar wasn't the one delivering he felt no sense of urgency.

"Oh! Donovan!" I said and greeted him with a hug. "Tamar had to show what's-his-name where Hailey is delivering. She should be back in a second. You know everyone, right?"

"Yeah. Hey, Camilla!" he waved to her and flashed a smile and then finished conversing with me. "I got home and noticed that all the gifts and stuff were still there. It was like you guys left right away, so I kinda put two and two together. Then I got the message from Tamar. How long have you guys been here?"

"A little over a half an hour," I told him. "Did you have time to put the food away?"

"Uhhh, hellooo?" Camilla clamored. "My water just broke over here!"

*   *   *   *

Hailey gave birth to a seven-pound, eight-ounce bundle of joy named Alex at about 10:38 p.m. He was too precious. Bryan was taking all sorts of photos of his bouncing baby boy. He called his parents and texted countless photos of the newborn and mother. He even sent a mass text to his co-workers at *The Post* and all of his blog and online social network followers.

Camilla had a longer labor and didn't deliver until early the next morning. Her six-pound, three-ounce, tiny munchkin made his appearance at about 1:37 a.m. She named him after her grandfather Gabriel.

Needless to say, the next day we all were pretty exhausted. As agreed, Bryan submitted blood samples for Camilla to determine if the child was his. He was reluctant because he wanted to enjoy the birth of his son, but he gave Camilla his word. He wanted to prove to her that he was not the father and wanted to be done with her once and for all. He had a new life with Hailey.

I suggested to Steve that he also provide a sample. Camilla had the right to know who her son's biological father was. Steve relented, but I persuaded him that there was no harm in doing so. He was more concerned with providing a sample for Alex. Bryan did not want to hear of it.

"Absolutely not. She's *my* fiancée!" Bryan told Steve. "Just because you couldn't close the deal gives you no right to even think Alex belongs to you!"

Steve looked at me before he spoke. He slightly shook his head and I grabbed his shoulder to calm him. I wasn't sure if he was going to use the arm I grabbed to take a swing at Bryan and send me flying across the room in the midst of the force of the punch, so I softly reminded him of what he told Ian.

"You said you were going to be cool."

"You're right, Josephine. You're right," he patted my hand lightly. "Bryan, man, I don't want any trouble. If Alex is mine, I just want to provide for him like I'm supposed to and see him whenever I can. I won't get in the way of you and Hailey's marriage."

"If she wanted you in her life, you'd be in it," he told Steve. "Just go away!"

"Punk ass," I overheard Ian say to Donovan.

"Bryan," I started, "it's not about you right now. It's about Alex, okay?"

Bryan took a moment and thought about what I said. He shook his head in one final protest, gave a heavy sigh of frustration and slightly shrugged.

"Fine," he surrendered.

*   *   *   *

Two months later, the results came back from both tests and I received calls from both Hailey and Camilla. Needless to say, we all were pretty shocked by the results. Camilla's son Gabriel, who, in my opinion looked a lot like her, was not Bryan's. Even though the condom broke on them that one time, the time she became pregnant didn't sync up quite accurately. She dodged a bullet there. However, her one night stand with Steve resulted in him impregnating her. Steve was not happy with the results, but he faced up to his responsibility and provided for little Gabriel and saw him as often as he could.

Bryan, on the other hand, was relieved that he was not the father of Camilla's son and told her three times in that one conversation when she told him that he knew it wasn't his. I think she said that he even chuckled and slightly celebrated. What an ass.

However, the next day, Bryan was sending out retractions to his family and co-workers and blog followers right after he called off the wedding with Hailey. I guess his love for her was overshadowed by the fact that Alex belonged to Steve. Apparently Bryan couldn't "close the deal" with Hailey either.

240 3958 1104
tnxietnx@hotmail.com

CPSIA information can be obtained at www.ICGtesting.com
264734BV00001B/4/P